Better than Happiness

Also by Gregory P. Smith

Out of the Forest

Better than Happiness

GREGORY P. SMITH

LIFE

PENGUIN LIFE

UK | USA | Canada | Ireland | Australia
India | New Zealand | South Africa | China

Penguin Life is part of the Penguin Random House group of companies
whose addresses can be found at global.penguinrandomhouse.com.

Penguin
Random House
Australia

First published by Penguin Life, 2023

Co-written with Craig Henderson
Cover illustrations by diane555/Getty Images
Cover design by Alex Ross Creative © Penguin Random House Australia Pty Ltd
Typeset in 13/18.5 pt Adobe Garamond by Midland Typesetters, Australia

Printed and bound in Australia by Griffin Press, an accredited
ISO AS/NZS 14001 Environmental Management Systems printer

A catalogue record for this
book is available from the
National Library of Australia

ISBN 978 1 76134 138 0

penguin.com.au

We at Penguin Random House Australia acknowledge that Aboriginal and Torres Strait Islander
peoples are the Traditional Custodians and the first storytellers of the lands on which we live
and work. We honour Aboriginal and Torres Strait Islander peoples' continuous connection to
Country, waters, skies and communities. We celebrate Aboriginal and Torres Strait Islander
stories, traditions and living cultures; and we pay our respects to Elders past and present.

For the lost, the damaged, the forgotten
and the lonely – and the little children
who dwell inside them.

CONTENTS

ABOUT THE AUTHOR

Gregory Peel Smith was born into a dysfunctional and abusive household in Tamworth, New South Wales, in 1955. His formative years were variously spent in a brutal Catholic orphanage, foster care and juvenile detention centres. He became homeless and was a rough sleeper for much of his adult life.

At thirty-five Gregory withdrew from the world to live in near total isolation in a rainforest in northern New South Wales. After ten years he finally emerged in 1999, close to death, to 'give society another chance'. Hampered by a poor education, Gregory set his sights on studying – first for a Certificate I in Information Technology at a community college, then for a bridging course at TAFE. In 2004 he began a degree in sociology at Southern Cross University.

Although he remained homeless during much of his studies, Gregory graduated in 2007 with first class honours.

In 2016 he was conferred with a PhD for his landmark research into the 'Forgotten Australians' – the estimated 500,000 people who, like him, suffered abuse in institutional out-of-home care during the twentieth century. Gregory was subsequently employed by Southern Cross University, where he is a research fellow, a senior lecturer in the social sciences and Chair of the Faculty of Business, Law and Arts Board.

Gregory is one of Australia's foremost lived experience experts in post-traumatic stress disorder, mental illness, domestic violence, alcohol and drug addiction, rough sleeping and homelessness. A sought-after public speaker and policy advisor, he is a specialist consultant to a number of government initiatives including the End Street Sleeping Collaboration: a New South Wales Premier's priority project to end street sleeping by 2030.

A leading advocate for the disenfranchised, disadvantaged and disconnected around the world, Gregory is a patron of numerous homeless vulnerability service providers in New South Wales and Queensland, and a global consultant for the Institute of Relational Health – a project run by CareSource in the United States to effect systems change in working with disadvantaged families. In 2023 he was awarded a Medal of the Order of Australia, honouring his service to the community through social welfare organisations.

Gregory's memoir *Out of the Forest* was published in 2018. Today he lives in Orange, New South Wales, with his partner, Catherine, their family and his beloved brood of chickens.

AUTHOR'S NOTE

A couple of years ago my partner, Catherine, jokingly referred to me as Benjamin Button. My searching expression must have said, 'I have no idea what you're talking about', so she explained that he is the titular character of a book about a man who ages in reverse. Unfortunately my body isn't matching that plot, but I understood Catherine's gag because, mentally, I most definitely feel like I was born old and am getting younger. At sixty-eight, my brain is functioning at a level I'd never thought possible: fresher and sharper than it has ever been. While that's pretty cool in itself, the most amazing part is it has happened in spite of my best efforts to utterly destroy my mind.

By the time I reached middle age, I'd obliterated an unspeakable number of brain cells through rampant substance abuse. Alcohol, opiates, hallucinogens, uppers, downers and anti-psychotics had all left their mark. Then there was the prowling pack of undiagnosed mental illnesses that tore at my cerebral faculties. Add to that a scant education, malnutrition, protracted social isolation and abysmal physical health, and it's no wonder I wound up chatting to aliens in the middle of a rainforest.

The damage was significant. My cognition was low and I suffered permanent memory loss, blackouts and frightening episodes of dissociation. Some of these problems plagued me for years after I returned to society following self-imposed exile, but I soldiered on the best I could. It wasn't until 2007 that I finally consulted with a psychologist, and that was at the insistence of Southern Cross University as a precondition of my doctorate. There was a concern that by researching the horrors of institutional care, and interviewing people who'd suffered in it, I might be retraumatised. That's how I got to know the psychologist Christina North. It was she who ultimately diagnosed me with severe depression, social anxiety and post-traumatic stress disorder.

In the sixteen years since then, we have both been struck by how far I've come emotionally, psychologically and intellectually. In the first couple of years post-forest, for example, I struggled to remember a person's name thirty seconds after being introduced to them. These days I easily memorise the names of fifty to sixty students every semester, in addition to their individual quirks, strengths and challenges.

I have increasingly developed the ability to identify, process and analyse detail in complex areas, too. In the world of academia I'm often told my thought processes are unique. My perspectives and interpretations, my contemporaries inform me, come from an unconventional place. I'm not doing anything wrong, they hasten to add, it's just that I think differently. I'm discovering that this is a valuable asset in academia, and it makes me very useful. Obviously, though, I don't recommend going on a journey such as mine as a method of reconfiguring your brain and starting a new career.

Christina North has a theory about why I'm wired differently. She believes that as my brain slowly recovered from decades of trauma and drug and alcohol abuse, I generated new neural pathways in order to bypass the damaged ones. Since a lot of this rewiring took place, unusually, in a higher-education setting, these neural connections resulted in the development of very refined and specialised mental skills. I have no other explanation for my bespoke brain function and, since I tend not to argue with Christina, I'm happy to accept hers.

I am fully aware, however, of what makes me unique when it comes to lived experience expertise. There are some excellent and well-qualified people with lived experience making great contributions in the fields of childhood trauma, substance abuse, social disadvantage, domestic violence, homelessness, out-of-home care and so on, but as far as I know, none have been exposed to the full spectrum to the extent that I have, and certainly not for as long. My qualifications were extremely hard won: nearly fifty years in the gaining.

It's richly ironic that such protracted and sustained disadvantage is now one of my strongest professional assets. In facing and managing myriad serious issues in life, I have developed a deep understanding of what the causes and effects are. I recognise the triggers and have mapped the fault lines, not just in myself but in others, as well as in society and government policy. I have stumbled into countless pitfalls and tumbled off a thousand wagons. I know where the demons like to lurk and where the hidden traps are set. I have seen a lot of people fall and founder and many others re-seed themselves and flourish.

It is important to understand that I am not a psychologist, psychiatrist, medical practitioner or even a drug and alcohol counsellor. However, I am a walking, talking encyclopedia of lived experience: a lot of them bad, many of them good, some quite ridiculous but all of them valuable. Some of the contents of this book may be triggering for some readers, and I urge anyone facing mental health or substance abuse issues to contact a GP or mental health professional.

Although I'm eminently qualified to discuss *my* lived experience and offer analysis and opinions on some grave and consequential subjects, I acknowledge everybody's lives are different, highly personal, diverse and complex. Some of my story might align with parts of yours, with people you know or not at all. Whatever the case, the stories and advice I share in the following pages come straight from the heart. Just as important – and arguably more so – is that I impart my optimism, too. I put it all forward humbly in the hope that even a fraction of it will help you have a better day and a better tomorrow.

PROLOGUE

'Are you happy?'

Three small words with the power to evoke big philosophical discussions. What is happiness, after all? I was never quite sure, but I can tell you categorically that it was thin on the ground in the house where I grew up. There wasn't any happiness to be found in the orphanage or the juvenile detention centres of my youth either. Yet, apparently, happiness was a very real thing and definitely worth striving for.

It was an intoxicating idea, the notion of a shimmering, gladdening prize at the end of an existential treasure hunt. The promise of these riches caused me to chase an elusive state of mind all over the place for forty-five fairly miserable years. After I was ejected from State care at nineteen, I searched feverishly for the smallest traces of happiness,

even in the most haunted corners of my dark and traumatised world.

I'd find it spasmodically, or at least I thought I did, often
swirling at the bottom of a schooner glass or smouldering at
the end of a joint. Later on I'd get injections of heroin happiness. Before long, just the anticipation of escaping into a
stoned or drunken state was enough to make me feel a little
bit golden. But of course, everything would fade back to
black soon enough and off I'd go, in hot pursuit of 'happy'
once again.

The allure of it sent me on physical wild goose chases
as well as the destructive chemical variety. As a young boy
I constantly ran away from home, chasing after the flipside
of sadness, and by the time I could drive a car these hopeful
excursions fanned out all over the map. Once I even tried to
drive four thousand kilometres across the continent for the
sake of feeling just a smidgen less awful.

It was 1982 and I'd quit my lowly job in Sydney. With
a few hundred dollars in my pocket, I pinned my hopes on a
happy new life in Perth. After drink-driving my way across
the baking Hay Plains, I made it as far as Adelaide before my
booze, petrol and optimism ran dry. I'd been homeless for
years at that point and was downing four litres of cheap cask
wine every day.

After a horrible night sleeping it off in my car, I found a phone booth, flipped through the *White Pages* and contacted a detox clinic in the City of Churches. For whatever long-forgotten reason, I was desperate for a lifeline. Blessedly, I was admitted as a patient later that day.

The staff prescribed medication in case I experienced delirium tremens – severe and potentially fatal alcohol withdrawal symptoms. The DTs, as they're known, usually start a few days after the last drink.

I have only fragmented memories of what happened next, but the following morning staff told me I'd gone into the DTs on the first night, before they'd had a chance to medicate me. They said I'd screamed and crashed about the room I was sharing with two other patients, overturning beds and diving for cover in a wide-eyed state of terror. Apparently I was fleeing from a phantom attacker who was trying to kill me with a spear. Later on I discovered 'delirium tremens' is Latin for 'trembling madness'.

After three weeks I walked out of detox in Adelaide sober and feeling on top of the world – so good, in fact, that I celebrated with a drink. A few days later I was back in the gutters of Sydney as drunk and as homeless as ever.

Up. Down. Up again. Down again. The pursuit of happiness was exhausting: a never-ending roller-coaster ride that

had long since ceased to be a thrill. After a few more tur-
bulent years of trauma and dysfunction, I decided I'd been
tossed around enough. Besides, I'd found another way to
escape from the anguish of my sorry life: it was in a quiet
place far removed from the heartless nation I believed had
judged and rejected me.

Around 1990, at the end of another long and pointless
trek to nowhere in particular, I wandered into a mountaintop rainforest in Goonengerry, northern New South Wales,
and stayed there for the best part of a decade.

During my tenure as a bush-dwelling hermit, I'd stare
into my campfire and contemplate why I was so angry,
alone, ashamed and so universally unhappy. I may have
been a homeless man and a drifter, but I had made repeated
attempts to find a meaningful place in society. The promise
of each new town and every new job, however, was broken
sooner or later. Why did I always fail? How come happiness
was always out of my reach?

Although I couldn't quite put my finger on it, I began to
wonder if something fundamental – something completely
unrelated to my severe and obvious problems – might also
be amiss.

'Is happiness even real? What does being happy actually mean?'

4

The answers would come, but not until much later.

When I left the forest and re-joined society in 1999, I was dismayed to find all the baggage I'd had before was still there waiting for me: the painful childhood trauma, the alcoholism and drug addiction, the loneliness and the contempt of an imperious society. After a remarkable park bench epiphany, I finally started to unpack it, piece by piece, hour by hour, week by week – a process that has lasted more than twenty-three years and continues today.

It has been a painstaking, beautiful, confronting, fascinating, terrifying and ultimately liberating journey. Along the way I have gained the education I was denied as a child. That process eventuated in me gaining a PhD and making a successful career in academia. As a social scientist I have not only developed a greater understanding of the human condition, but I have been gifted the opportunity to share my knowledge and experiences with others.

I have also come to realise something I wish I'd known a long time ago: happiness is completely overrated.

I still wind up in detox clinics from time to time, but nowadays it's in answer to a call for help, not the other way around. As a lived experience expert in alcoholism, addiction and PTSD, I'm often invited to speak to people who are in the throes of detoxification and rehabilitation. Many have been homeless, too — another tie that binds us.

I don't preach. People's problems are varied and complex, and a speech from me won't fix a lifetime of woe. All I can do is tell them how *I* went about transitioning out of trauma, addiction and chronic long-term homelessness into a rich and fulfilling life surrounded by people I love and who love me.

While you may not be going through anything as extreme as detox or homelessness, the chances are, if you've picked up this book, there are things about your life you'd like to change. I'm not going to preach to you either, but the subtext is pretty clear: 'If I can do it, so can you.'

Usually I speak to people in detox centres in groups. I tell them about my life for forty minutes or so and then do my best to answer their questions. The most common question by far is: 'Are you happy?'

It's a sad question when posed in the hallways of healing, and it speaks to the misery of people battling addiction, sadness and a lack of hope. The fact is that happiness is impermanent: it can vanish like smoke in the wind. It is not an answer to life's problems nor a lasting reward for better choices. I don't even consider it an ideal state of mind.

So whenever I'm asked the question, I always give the same answer:

> *'There's a realm beyond happiness that very few people inhabit. Follow what I've done, and you may one day enter it. It's a wonderful place called contentment.'*

This is the story of how I got there.

CHAPTER ONE

TO HELL AND BACK

The expression 'to hit rock bottom' is used to describe any number of personal nadirs: divorce, the loss of a job, depression, grief over the death of a loved one. I hear it *a lot* in some of the circles I move in today, especially in relation to substance abuse. The term was popularised in the middle of last century by the Alcoholics Anonymous movement and posits that there's a point in life so low that there is simply no further to fall. The thinking is the only direction you can go from rock bottom is up. I can assure you it's not.

Homeless, destitute and frightfully damaged, I'd landed at the bottom long before I lived in the forest (where, funnily enough, I made my bed on a rock). It was part of the reason I withdrew into the wilderness in the first place, and the change elevated me, for a while anyway.

The sense of relief and security that came from leaving the society I felt had shunned me from birth made me feel my life was actually improving for once. There was no one around to hurt me and no one to judge me. Being surrounded by natural beauty twenty-four seven was a gratifying distraction from my inner tribulations, too. But after a year or so the illusion ended. Mental anguish and abject solitude do not a happy hermit make. I crashed back down so hard I broke through rock bottom and kept going into whatever lies beneath. I'm not a religious person, but I'll call it hell – and I lived in it for years.

Stooped and needing a stick to walk, I finally staggered out of the Goonengerry forest on 22 November, 1999. It had been a case of re-enter society or die up on the mountain. I chose life and was promptly hit by a car on my first day back in the world. Lismore Hospital's record of the aftermath is the only reason I know the date of my re-emergence. Although moderately banged up by the car, I was already physically and mentally ruined. I was psychotic and skeletally malnourished. My medical records show I weighed 41.6 kg.

After a few weeks in a rehabilitation centre I was stabilised, patched up and released like rescued wildlife back into society. Although social workers at the rehab centre had organised for me to receive a disability support pension to get me on my feet, I immediately faced a major stumbling block – I had no idea how to stand up and take my place in the world, let alone walk a new path.

At forty-five I was still homeless, still traumatised and still filled with anger, hurt and sorrow. I remained a chronic alcoholic and a drug addict, too, and I felt more alone in the universe than ever before. As I contemplated this state of affairs one sunny afternoon on a park bench in Tweed Heads, I wondered what might come *after* hell.

I had my life's possessions with me: an old backpack stuffed with some clothes and knick-knacks, plus a bottle of bourbon, cask wine, Drum tobacco, marijuana and a gram of cocaine – the bitter fruits of a misspent pension. Sorely depressed and ashamed, I began to weep as a particularly heartbreaking thought entered my mind:

'If only I had one person to tell all my problems to, things might be alright.'

What happened next can be hard for people to get their heads around. In a way, I suppose, I discovered what comes after hell – at least in my experience. To my enduring surprise and gratitude, it was a place that eventually led me to a deep and clear understanding of myself and, ultimately, to my salvation.

The moment the painful longing for just one friend drifted into my consciousness I experienced a full-blown vision as lucid as any waking event in my life. I was no longer slumped against the backpack on the park bench, but standing on a smouldering battlefield, scattered with the ruins of an abysmal life and holding a double-edged sword. Tense and ready for combat, I held the weapon aloft in anticipation of the next fight when . . .

Absolutely nothing happened.

I waited and then waited some more on the hazy, barren plains of lifelong conflict, primed to swipe at the enemy with the heavy blade – but still nothing happened. No army appeared on the horizon, not a single foe rushed forward. That's when it dawned on me:

'I am the enemy. I have caused all of this destruction. It's been me all along.'

For close to half a century I had been fighting myself, and finally it was time to stop.

When the vision ended, I was back on my bum on the park bench. Overcome with a feeling of pure grace and determination, I rose and walked away, leaving the backpack full of poison behind. I committed that I would never drink alcohol, take drugs or smoke cigarettes again for as long as I lived. The fighting was over: I would do no more harm – to myself or anyone else – and I would strive to be the very best person I could. Always.

These were the first footfalls in an arduous uphill quest for sobriety that I'll tell you more about in the next chapter. In turn these steps sent me on a life-changing odyssey of self-discovery and personal growth beyond anything I'd ever thought possible. It was a long, hard road. Suffice to say, stopping drinking and drugging didn't suddenly solve my problems – not even close – but it did clear a little spot on the filthy windscreen of my life to peer through, just enough to begin to assess the damage and ponder the kind of person I might one day become.

Working out where your next drink is coming from and getting on with the business of obliteration is sort of like having a job, in that it accounts for most of your day. An early dividend from abstinence was the huge tracts of time I suddenly had on my hands. It allowed me to slow down a bit and gave me scope for some unpolluted self-reflection – something I'd eschewed all my life.

I slept rough in the beachside dunes around the New South Wales–Queensland border, which was fairly familiar ground to me, and hung around the local soup kitchens. I tried to kick-start a working life, but my ambition was far greater than my ability. In those early post-forest days I was so physically and mentally messed up that I was unemployable. Just making it through each hour without drinking took a huge amount of effort and wit, but I became aware I was thinking more clearly than I had in decades.

I'd sit for hours and replay the epiphany over and over in my mind. I was convinced there were important lessons to be learned and perhaps even some directions on a new way of living. I realised one of the core revelations was about what I came to know as acceptance. Up until that point in my life, I had always tried to have things my own way. I focused all of my resentment, anger and disappointment on the external world, which, conveniently, meant I didn't have to look inward for answers or someone to blame.

I had never been able to see – let alone accept – that I was the problem. This immature mindset had deep roots in my defective childhood.

Over the first few weeks of my new life, as I wandered around Tweed Heads and the Gold Coast trying to consolidate my modest psychological progress, I fixated on the word 'acceptance'. Mentally, I was on foreign ground. While I'd accepted, on the face of it, that my most destructive battles had been internal and that my deepest wounds had been self-inflicted, what was I supposed to do with that understanding?

> *'What is the value of acceptance? What does it mean? How is it gained? How is it exercised? What else do I need to accept? How will it benefit me?'*

In the beginning, the only thing I was certain of was the importance of the concept. I accepted that I was in the dunes and homeless, and that my ambitions for a better life would take time to eventuate. Life felt a fraction easier with acceptance being actioned. As I steadily dried out, I even experienced some little moments of bliss and astoundment: watching a bee caress yellow petals in a council garden or just feeling gentler in my soul. I wanted more.

The A-word bubbled up, unbidden, from my past. I'd been on the fringes of enough Alcoholics Anonymous meetings over the years to be familiar with key lines from the Serenity Prayer, which was invariably pinned to the wall of whatever church hall I happened to roll into. Although AA was never for me and I don't rely on it now, the prayer came to mind regardless:

> *'God grant me the serenity to accept the things I cannot change,*
> *Courage to change the things I can,*
> *And the wisdom to know the difference . . .'*

Having been beaten and terrorised in Catholic institutions, I have zero faith in deities, so the very first thing I accepted was that there were parts of the prayer I didn't need to buy into. To me the recitation wasn't a revelation, comfort or a rallying cry – but it *was* food for thought. For one thing, I noticed 'serenity' and 'acceptance' were mentioned in the same line. A little serenity sounded good.

Although I was drug free and abstinent, I remained in constant conflict with my environment and those who populated it. These 'externals' could stir up intense anger and bitterness, and lead to harsh judgements and baleful looks from me. I didn't like the things people said, I couldn't stand how people carried themselves and I hated how they dressed.

Anyone in a suit was a problem. I considered the well-attired to be smug corporate know-alls. There'd been an explosion in the availability and affordability of mobile phones during my time as a recluse, and the suits could be relied on to stand out in the street and talk extra loud into theirs. This was the height of performative nonsense, if you asked me. If I wanted to make a phone call, I'd go somewhere really quiet where no one could hear me – not that I had a phone or anyone to ring.

Certain haircuts stoked anger and swift judgement in the court of Gregory, too. The suits all wore a short back and sides – the omnipresent hairdo of the State that had been forced on me in the boys' homes. Every time I passed a suit with my wild, dreadlocked mane flapping in the breeze I'd think, 'What a dickhead! Grow your hair and show a little bit of personality!'

For decades I had rebuffed what I perceived as society's attempts to make demands on me, and in the process I had mistaken my internal battles for exterior conflict. I believed society wanted me to conform, to marry me off, to see that I had 2.5 children and a home with a picket fence. It wanted me shorn with short back and sides like the sheep in their collars and ties.

In the past I had assuaged this endless seething about society, suits, haircuts and picket fences by getting blind drunk and hiding behind my enormous beard in my rainforest lair. Out here in the world though – abstinent from alcohol and attempting to be an actual member of the human race – I couldn't self-medicate so easily against my anger and resentment. Eventually I had to face what was causing it.

In thinking it through during aimless walks and wakeful nights in the dunes, I realised I had never accepted that I don't have control over other people, and my anger was an emotion born of this misconception. Finally recognising that I was powerless over others was a lightbulb moment. When it dawned on me, I stretched out on the sand and mentally drafted a personal statement of intent:

'Anything that exists outside of me – anything that I don't control – I need to be able to accept. I might not like it, but in the process of accepting I should see a corresponding settlement of conflict within me.'

So much easier said than done. I had to remind myself daily, if not hourly, to walk my new talk. Early on in this hopeful new phase of life, I also began to understand the value of seeing things differently. I forced myself to change the way I looked at each day: to slow right down and appreciate the little things. In taking the time to absorb each moment, I became aware of how grateful I was for a cup of tea or a piece of toast at the soup kitchens. Being slower and more thoughtful changed my overall demeanour, too. Where in the past I would react to the events of the day, I was beginning to *respond* to them instead.

I also adjusted the way I viewed myself. One of the traits I recognised early on was the unreasonable and unhelpful way I made demands of others and the universe – from things as simple as 'Let your hair grow, dickhead!' to complex matters like why I felt entitled to my deep-seated stubbornness and arrogance.

In my early days of homelessness, I would look up from the gutter, envious of the passing office workers and wonder if I might one day get a job in a glass building too. By the time I was thirty, though, I'd taken to scoffing at the people who toiled in skyscrapers. Rather than aspire to a career of my own, or even look up from that lowly place, I regarded the gutter as a podium from where I could pass judgement on the masses. I had nothing but contempt for a stupid and compliant population, enslaved to boring lives and in thrall to commercial routines. At least that's what I told myself. More often than not, I just felt small down there on the footpath, like I was perched on the edge of a cigarette paper, swinging my legs, but too stubborn to admit I was the cause of my being there.

In recognising that these were self-defeating behaviours, it began to dawn on me how obnoxious I had been for so long. For decades I had been a wholly unpleasant person who was extremely difficult to get on with. That's quite a thing to realise about oneself. I tried not to make excuses or justify my past attitudes and conduct, but rather simply accept that they had been a part of who I was. This allowed me to ask a watershed question:

'Do I want to keep them or change them?'

It was a no brainer. In the process of unravelling my tangled and knotted worldview, I also came to realise that I hated – and I mean *really hated* – any kind of demand being made of me. I could trace those roots back to childhood too. In the orphanage where my mother abandoned me at ten, and in the juvenile jails the courts sent me to as a teenager, the demands came thick and fast. 'Stand up. Wash now. Shut up. Sit down. Sleep now. Get up. Eat now.'

Recognising my disdain for this, I rationalised that if I didn't like people making demands on me, maybe

I shouldn't make demands on them. That's not to say I didn't need things from other humans, society and the universe. It just meant I had to alter my approach. Maybe I could ask rather than demand?

The terms of this new outlook were simple: I could ask but, as with all requests, the final decision was not up to me and I would always accept the outcome. This was a big help in alleviating the frustration I felt in my fruitless attempts to find work.

In all my years I had never risen above unskilled jobs like cleaning, factory work or gardening. After ten years as a hermit, however, I couldn't get a single interview – let alone a knockback – for even the lousiest positions I applied for.

Rather than get upset at my lack of control, I released my grip and left the outcome to the grace of the universe. Sometimes it was difficult to take, and I had to work harder at getting to a point of acceptance. By doing so over time, however, it grew less upsetting and disheartening to accept that I was unemployed and homeless – for the time being at least.

This rudimentary work around acceptance represented the first time in my life I had taken a look at my attitude, even though plenty of others – from teachers, to jailers, to random men in pubs – had offered their views on it plenty of times: 'You've got a rotten attitude, Smith!' Those were words I'd heard a million times. My standard response to such observations was either a barrage of bile or a savage headbutt to the face. If you didn't like my attitude, you could go and get stuffed.

Our personalities and our worldviews are formed by the confluence of many disparate factors, but a huge amount of who we are and how we present to the world comes down to our attitudes towards everything and everyone around us. I'd never considered I had the need – let alone the power – to change any of mine.

As I consolidated my focus on becoming a better man, I realised that acceptance was in fact an attitude and, since I'd begun to shift the dial on that, I'd become familiar with the notion of 'self'. Changing an attitude requires constant effort and vigilance. Any time I felt myself drifting into conflict by yielding to unhelpful attitudes of the past, I'd yank on my lead as you would an aggressive dog:

'Self! Back off! This is out of your realm. Just accept it and focus on something else.'

One of the things that really got me going were queues in supermarkets. My idea of a good shop was to get in, grab the few things I needed and get the hell back out – the quicker, the better. Not everyone, however, shared my sense of urgency. It was when I reached the check-out phase of the excursion that the problems usually began.

To begin with, most of the check-outs would be closed, which forced us hapless shoppers into conga lines of consumerism that snaked away from the one or two counters that were open. By the time I reached the penultimate position in the queue, my patience would be bottoming out. Already agitated and fidgety, the universe would purposefully play with me by having the shopper in front of me strike up a fascinating conversation with the check-out person. My toes would start to tap, and weight transfers from one leg to the other would commence.

'Mate, settle down!' I'd remind myself. *'We're just shopping. You can't control everyone. If they want to chat, that's okay.'*

I would try to remember how fortunate I was to be able to afford food in the first place and that the country I lived in was littered with massive buildings stocked full of everything we needed to survive. Usually that worked, but sometimes there was a caveat: if the ice cream melted, I'd leave it on the counter.

Another challenge I had to face in the beginning was the fact that I remained an outsider, emotionally as well as physically. By reminding myself to accept that I was lonely for the time being, I was able to focus inwardly in a gentler way than ever before. I began to feel gratitude for the gift of life and the promises it was wrapped in. Each morning I'd wake in the dunes and mentally prepare myself for the day ahead. Even if it was pouring with rain and I was soaked to the skin, my first thought was, *'Thank you for another beautiful day.'* Every dawn had become special because it presented another opportunity to exercise the power to make better choices.

I'd forensically tidy up my camp, remove all trace of my existence and accept the strong possibility that I'd end the day without exchanging a single word with another human being. I'd ride on buses, walk the foreshores and sit in parks or in soup kitchens, listening in silence to other peoples' conversations. Even when I'd enter a shop to buy a drink, there was a good chance I wouldn't speak.

In some ways my new existence was an echo of how I used to walk in the forest. Back then I'd traverse the same trails over and over, getting to know the different critters and where they liked to hang out. I'd see the same trees, palms, logs and boulders, and I could place them with my eyes closed. In the same way, I began to notice the people who caught the same buses, visited the soup kitchens and followed the same trails in the metropolitan forest. Where I used to identify different lichen or moss on trees and rocks up in Goonengerry, I began to observe similarities in the humans I encountered each day. Some, I noticed, smelled heavily of alcohol whenever our paths crossed. Others had red eyes or dilated pupils at different times, depending on which part of the day we passed each other by. Reflecting on this, I'd wonder what pain these people were trying to kill.

These observations helped me form ideas about how I wanted to change. I did it without judgement, because I'd lived that life, too. One thing we still shared was loneliness, and I didn't want to be lonely anymore.

Accepting loneliness was not easy. As my life stabilised little by little, I found ongoing isolation harder to bear, particularly because I passed by hundreds, maybe even thousands, of people every day. Sometimes my mind would drift back to my bed of ferns by the fire in the forest, and I would contemplate a return to Goonengerry, only to yank on the dog leash and remind myself of the vows I'd made on the park bench.

During my last days in the forest, I'd reached a point where I felt like the only thing I had left to lose was my life. I had been quite okay with that, because it would have meant an end to the misery, the pain, the self-loathing and a lifetime of failure. After my great awakening, however, I discovered I had far more than just my life to give: I had my word and my name, too.

Rarely had I kept my word to myself or anyone else. The smouldering battlefield of my epiphany was strewn with the wreckage of a thousand broken promises. I made the decision that day to never again say I'd do something unless I truly intended to finish it. I started small – just getting through the day without tripping up.

'Today I'm not going to have a drink, drugs or a cigarette.'

Only after making that solemn morning promise would I go about the business of my day. Sometimes the agenda was very simple, like finding somewhere to wash my face or get a feed. Other times I had no business at all outside of sitting in the dunes and watching the waves roll in. When I closed my eyes at night, however, I'd be mentally exhausted from the Herculean effort I'd put in to not drinking, smoking or getting stoned. The end of each day was another precious promise kept. When I look back now, it's incredible how far from those sand dunes my word has taken me.

My name precedes me nowadays. In the orphanage everyone called me Greg. I had always hated that, but even more so when it was an unwanted label the Catholic nuns had slapped on me. In the boys' homes my name was either replaced by a number or dismissively reduced to 'Smith'. During my years in the forest I assumed the mythical, mystical alias William H. Power, or Will Power. The H stood for 'Higher'.

In my new life I wanted to step away from those names, not to bury or deny the memories – because they're important to me – but to establish who I wanted to be. So I became Gregory. Gregory is who I remain and always will. People who know me will call me Gregory. Those who don't will inevitably call me Greg, or even Smithy.

Like flexing a muscle, my attitude of acceptance developed and strengthened over time, and it remains an important part of my psyche. It was the first major step in my journey of self-discovery and self-determination. And laying that foundation led to another realisation that would in turn place another brick in the formation of a new me – the principle that, as long as it didn't impact me, what other people did was none of my business.

This didn't only relate to my useless judgements about neat hair and spiffy clothes. It addressed my long history of being a slave to other peoples' emotions. In the past, every time someone expressed negative emotions towards me, my own cauldron would boil over. I was just as likely to respond to a garden variety jibe like, 'What are *you* looking at?' with a shoulder charge, a fist in the face or a vicious verbal attack.

It was such a relief to finally understand that other people's crap didn't matter and certainly didn't require a spray or a headbutt from me. Their loves, hates, choices, political views, peccadillos and philosophies – right down to their favourite colours – were matters solely for them. I didn't have to buy into any of it, and not doing so saved a huge amount of emotional energy.

Ever so gradually, the spring of my changing outlook spilled into other parts of my being where more green shoots began to show. Although my track record for keeping promises had been abysmal, I'd always felt I possessed a certain amount of integrity. Given the option to tell the truth or a lie, I almost always went with the truth, and I had an expectation that others should live by the same standard. Of course when they didn't, I'd feel angry, disappointed and resentful – a clear sign that my attitude needed adjusting, too.

'I wonder if I should lower my expectations?'

I ended up going one better: in my new life I would place *no* expectations on people. If someone did what they said they were going to do, awesome! A bonus! If they didn't though, or if they lied or deceived me, I hadn't emotionally invested in the outcome in the first place, so there was no harm done.

This was an amazing development and it led to a fundamental change in the way I considered other people. I still hadn't one friend in the world, but by dropping expectations I began placing the various people I encountered around the soup kitchens and other homeless haunts into separate categories. If a person behaved badly, I didn't judge them; I just moved them into a different column from those who acted with integrity. It was the beginning of what I would come to know as discernment – an important life skill when choosing friends, and something that had been completely lacking in my life.

Over the course of a few months, these new ideas took root in me and began to grow. A lot of the old traits, however, were not easily weeded out – particularly my lifelong companions anger and resentment.

Leaving the rainforest had been a massive shock to the system. I'd traded a serene, beautiful environment for a dirty place where artificial light, machine noise, litter and the fossil fuel stench of society permeated every nook and cranny. Even though I'm deaf in my left ear, I found noise pollution the hardest to adjust to. Everywhere I went I could hear the electricity humming in substations and overhead wires: an awful sound of industrial power feeding the desires of society. In my old life the low-frequency drone would have literally sent me running for the hills.

By reminding myself to accept that I had no control over pollution – or, indeed, the electricity grid – and acknowledging it is a by-product of modern society, I slowly grew more comfortable living in the organised mess. I can still hear the buzz of electricity today, but I've managed to turn the volume down on it.

Despite the culture shock, I noticed parallels between my new urban existence and my years in the bush. Living – illegally – in a state forest was a closely guarded subterfuge that required me to follow the path of least resistance. If I didn't, I'd find myself in conflict with my surrounds: I'd upend leaves, break twigs, leave boot prints in moss, disturb rocks and the undergrowth, and thereby leave clues to my whereabouts.

I found it just as important to follow the path of least resistance in the concrete jungle, too, although the aim was to mesh with society, not hide from it. If I encountered conflict along whatever emotional or interpersonal route I was heading down, I needed to stop, assess my surrounds and what was happening inside me, and change course. If I was *still* meeting resistance on the path, then I was clearly going in completely the wrong direction. Over time I turned conflict into a compass.

Navigating life in that way has served me well and seen me traverse a lot of ground – from the sand dunes, bus stops and soup kitchens of the Gold Coast and Tweed region to having a home of my own and a meaningful place in the world.

Acceptance has remained a good friend, too. In more than twenty years of practising it, the attitude has had a major and enduring impact on me, bringing both peace of mind and purpose. Acceptance is not to be confused with unconditional surrender. Acceptance is not saying 'I can't question', 'I can't discuss', 'I can't find a better way'. It's about *how* we approach and manage the problems in our lives. I learned that just accepting 'what is' at certain times in my life has given me more power to change the things I don't like.

In some ways it's a paradox: to change something we first have to accept it for what it is. Only through accepting my perceived flaws and limitations could I see that there were pathways to improvement. The same applied when it came to learning to accept one of the biggest conundrums in my life: the man in the mirror.

For as long as I can recall, I hated who I was, right down to how I looked. I'd been told it so many times that I truly believed I was the ugliest person that ever lived. The main reason I became so comfortable with a giant beard in adult life was because I couldn't bear to look in a mirror to shave. That's a lot of shame and sadness to carry around, so during my hermit years, I just dropped it. I completely gave up on caring about myself. For years I was unkempt, unwashed, undernourished and unbelievably unhealthy, not that I could see it, because I flatly refused to look at my reflection. Left unchecked, that attitude would have resulted in my early death. Self-acceptance is the main reason I am not only here today but able to look myself in the mirror – not that I want to shave now, either.

In 2016 I was at a doctor's surgery for a minor skin complaint. He gave me some medication and as he was checking me over, he said, 'I can improve your face a little bit if you like. Just a couple of touch-ups with your chin and nose.'

I stared back at him in mock horror. 'Mate, it's taken me sixty-one years to accept who I am,' I exclaimed. 'I don't want to change that now!'

I cannot overstate the role that having an attitude of acceptance has played in turning my life around. It was a huge first step and a crucial factor in the most important struggle I faced after leaving the forest: getting sober and drug free for good.

CHAPTER TWO

NONE FOR THE ROAD

When I left the park bench, I walked straight into a world of temptation. It didn't matter that I didn't own a TV, a computer or even a transistor radio – the multi-billion-dollar advertising spend of the alcohol conglomerates reached me down on the pavement all the same.

Incitement to drink was writ large on the sides of pubs. It was in a newspaper on the footpath, open to a page of wine and spirits specials. It echoed in the discarded stubbies in the beachside parks and a drained bourbon bottle marooned on the sand. It cooed to me from a bus shelter ad for champagne and sparkled off a vodka can flattened by cars on a zebra crossing. The signals came from every direction, and they all wanted me to fail.

Alcohol flushes out of your system within a couple of days: not so the incessant waves of anguish, anxiety and craving. In the sudden absence of inebriation, the chemical urges to get drunk were constant. Sometimes they felt almost physical, like an invisible finger prodding me in the back. The pining for booze forced me to ponder how a future without it would require me to come to terms with the way in which alcoholism and addiction had impacted every facet of my existence.

I was around twenty-five when I first knew I had a problem with alcohol. Although I didn't start drinking in earnest until I was nineteen or twenty (you couldn't drink in the boys' homes), I very quickly recognised the crude analgesic effect alcohol had over the psychological injuries of childhood. I dived into the bottle headfirst.

I hadn't been introduced to drugs yet, but the signs that I'd become an alcoholic were plain and clear. I'd drink regularly and copiously, and either grow violent or pass out cold before I had the chance to provoke a fight. If I was employed and payday rolled around, I'd drink every last dollar I had and go hungry for the rest of the week. A strong indicator that I had a serious issue? When alcohol took precedence over food.

If you've ever wondered whether or not you're an alcoholic, ask yourself if you hide bottles. In other words, do you drink on your own and in secret? Does drinking interfere with your ability to work? Does it cause you legal, social, financial or relationship problems? Are you constantly thinking about it and planning your next appointment with a drink? I ticked all the boxes.

Drugs came a little later in life. What started with a toke on a joint outside a pub ended with galloping addictions to marijuana, heroin, cocaine, amphetamines and literally any kind of pharmaceutical I could get my hands on. Drugs made me feel good at first: I loved escaping into an altered state, where reality was obscure and distraction was assured. If drugs happened to kill my internal pain along the way, even better. Staying numb to the reality of daily life, where I was stalked by shame and guilt, was the main event.

No matter what kind of pain and sickness alcoholism brought me, I could never break free. If I had to get up and go to work after a messy night, I'd be so full of remorse, so sick and defeated, that I'd swear I'd never drink again. I'd stumble off to whatever lowly job I had picking fruit or sweeping floors, feeling like death. After a couple of hours, the heavy skies of the hangover would start to lift. By lunch-time I'd be feeling not too bad and come mid-afternoon I'd be entertaining the thought of hitting the pub again.

At knock-off time I'd borrow $20 off someone and the next thing I'd know I'd be a few beers in and numb again with the party starting up in my head. I'd find a way to get even more pissed until I blacked out or got knocked out. I would cut the black-printed coasters into small tablet-like shapes and sell them as acid trips. Of course, I couldn't spend the profits of these scams in the same venue. By morning I'd be back where I started out twenty-four hours earlier. If the definition of insanity is doing the same thing over and over and expecting a different result, then I was certifiable.

Drinking and violence went hand in hand, not only because I'd lose control of my temper but because they were components of the same coping mechanism. I would seek out violence in the same way some people cut themselves to get relief and externalise internal pain. My preferred method of self-mutilating was to pick a fight. Usually I'd target the biggest bloke in the pub, and if there wasn't a hefty enough guy in the vicinity, I'd stir up trouble with a group of men.

Guess who always came off worst? My bare-knuckle approach to processing inner pain left me perennially bruised and covered in grazes. Split lips, loose teeth, black eyes and bleeding noses were common, too, and I wound up in hospital a few times with a concussion or requiring a needle and thread. Today I have a large collection of faded scars as souvenirs of the mayhem.

My most alarming expression of self-harm occurred one night when I was twenty-nine. Instead of brawling in a pub, I deliberately set fire to a house in Tamworth, with the full knowledge someone was inside it. That poor soul was me. I was saved by some valiant firefighters before the flames could take me and was subsequently charged with arson, maliciously setting fire to a dwelling and recklessly endangering human life – mine.

I was looking down the barrel of years in prison, and I spent the next twelve months sorrowfully wending my way through the court system. Not long before I was due to face trial, a psychiatrist intervened and my defence managed to have the charges dismissed on mental health grounds. I was prescribed anti-depressants and mind-numbing anti-psychotic drugs, which I gobbled daily for the next year. Before long I resumed my drinking and drugging, too, and stuck with it all the way to the park bench battlefield in Tweed Heads.

It wasn't until I stopped drinking that I realised that the emotional grave where I'd hastily buried my problems was pathetically shallow. In the cold, pale dawn of abstinence, a lot of horrors from my past were resurrected and I would have to face all of them.

The priority, however, was staying away from drink and drugs, including the evil nicotine. I'd spent a lifetime fighting myself, and mind-altering chemicals had greased the gears of my internal war machine. Far from acting as painkillers, they actually prolonged and intensified my suffering.

Unlike a lot of people who try to get sober, I resolved to do it alone. I didn't consult a doctor, let alone drug and alcohol counsellors or qualified support networks, and Alcoholics Anonymous had never been for me. I didn't eschew professional help out of arrogance; I was just too disillusioned with society after ten years removed from it to place any trust in the mainstream.

Today, I recognise what a gamble that was. If you've been drinking very heavily for a long time and you really want to stop, I strongly recommend you see a doctor and do it through a detox program. I had suffered DTs in the past – terrifying experiences – and I was extremely lucky not to develop a full-blown case by going cold turkey post-epiphany, particularly considering I experienced some low-level hallucinations in the first few days of abstinence.

*

A small but noisy part of me continued to resent the fact that I'd left the forest and was putting myself through this misery. In realising that my very best thinking had led me to the world's loneliest park bench, however, I recognised I needed to do more than think – I had to act. The first concrete action I took was to physically separate myself from my cache of drugs and alcohol: to stand up and literally walk away from that life.

'Okay. Done. So what have I got for a second act?'

Friendless and wary of professional help, I had only my instincts to rely on. The one tangible thing I could think to do was coach myself between the ears. I began by reciting the words, 'I don't drink and I don't do drugs, no matter what,' over and over again on a loop.

Day after day, week after week, I'd repeat variations of this mantra around the clock. Resting in the sand dunes: *'I don't drink, I don't smoke and I don't take drugs.'*

Riding on a bus: *'My name is Gregory and I don't drink alcohol.'*

Walking down the street: *'I don't drink and I don't do drugs. I'm Gregory and I just don't drink. No matter what.'*

These weren't just affirmations to distract myself and deflect the cravings, they constituted another 'action' to help me succeed. By gently chanting encouragement to myself, even when I wasn't being challenged, I was strengthening my resolve for the inevitable times I would be vulnerable – when I really, *desperately* felt like a drink or a drug. If I learned my lines by rote, I figured my default response would become automatic.

'No! I don't drink and I don't do drugs.'

Alcohol's grip had been so tight that it squeezed me on a deep subconscious level, too. More than once I dreamed I'd gotten drunk and started smoking again – a dreadful, depressing thought steeped in failure and shame. The nightmares were so vivid and powerful that it would take days to convince myself they weren't real, that I was still abstinent and that my word had held.

I can't say I recognised it at the time, but over the years I've identified that for alcoholics there are three types of saying 'No':

1 When you're miles from anywhere and have no access to alcohol or drugs: it's easy to refuse because, even if you feel the urge, you simply can't follow through.

2 When you're invited: somebody's got a bottle and you're offered a drink. It can be a hell of a temptation and it's crucial to be able to default to 'no' straight away. This is where the practice pays off.

3 When autonomous opportunities arise: you feel like a drink and you're standing across the road from the pub with a pocket full of money. That's the ultimate test. It's not you versus the pub, it's you versus you. Which part of your being is going to win? I'm not a gambler, but if I were, I'd always back the horse who'd been learning their lines. *'I don't drink. Ever.'*

In the early days of abstinence I'd walk away from those tussles outside the pub feeling ten feet tall, but I soon realised there was danger in the hubris. I'd be on such an emotional high that a few hours later I'd crash back down. While I'd trained hard to win the initial mental skirmish, I was unprepared for when the thrill of victory faded. When it did, time and time again, the attendant depression was amplified by the knowledge that I couldn't do the things I used to do to kill the pain.

By the time I'd won my umpteenth kerbside showdown, the waves of physical cravings had weakened a little, but the battle continued to rage in the arena of the mind. To help me prevail there, I made sure I had something to do every day, be it a trip to a new soup kitchen or poring over job ads on public noticeboards and in the newspaper. Each night I'd map out a schedule to keep me occupied the next day. The more prepared I was the better. If I was catching a bus, for example, I always took something to try to read. I was not a good reader and found it difficult to pronounce the words in my mind. Often I would try to articulate them out loud if no one was around. Interestingly that's how I realised I needed glasses: drugs and alcohol had even prevented me from seeing that I couldn't see! I bought some cheap specs from a service station and stuck with the plan.

I was learning that there's no quick fix to alcoholism or addiction. It takes effort, time, concentration and vigilance. Still, I wasn't drinking and although I hadn't transitioned to a wonderful new life at breakneck speed, I definitely wasn't going backwards either. Had I reached a place from where the only way was up?

As I recited my mantras and started to see things in sharper focus, I decided to set some meaningful emotional goals for myself – for the first time in my life. One was to reconnect with my family. My parents had died years before, but I didn't know much about what had become of my little sisters or my teenage daughter, Katie.

I'd become estranged from my five sisters after I fell into homelessness. When we were little kids, however, four of the girls had suffered alongside me at the hands of our violent parents and later at St Patrick's Orphanage in Armidale. Now adults, I imagined my sisters had their own problems to deal with. I had no address or contact details for any of them.

As for Katie, she was born in 1986 during a particularly grim period of my life. Her mother, Nicola, and I had gotten together while I was facing jail on the arson charges. We lived in a caravan, drank excessively and took a lot of drugs. One day I came home to find Katie and her mother gone. Years later Nicola took her own life.

Mentally ill and untethered in the wake of my near misses with suicide and jail, I'd only managed to spend minimal time with Katie, partly due to my own dysfunction and partly due to the State's restrictions on my access to her. I had never given up hope of forming a relationship with Katie, and her face was one of the bright things I could see through that clean little space on the windshield of my soul.

I asked the social workers in the soup kitchens I frequented how I might go about finding her. Someone suggested the Salvation Army, so I phoned them, explained the situation and gave them Katie's name. About a week later I got a phone call: they'd found her and she was living only one hundred kilometres away!

I wasn't just happy, I was on a stratospheric emotional high . . . for a few hours, anyway. Back in the sand dunes that night, I mentally flipped through the Rolodex of damage I'd done to Katie by being a deeply damaged and mostly missing father. From pure elation to shame and depression in the space of one afternoon.

'I can't keep living like this.'

The next day I swallowed hard and phoned her. Katie was going on sixteen, living somewhere in Lismore, working at Domino's Pizza and studying at TAFE. Although I didn't know what to expect, I was heartened when she not only agreed to speak to me, she was happy for me to come and visit her. Thanks to a broken-down car, however, my first attempt was aborted. When we spoke on the phone again to arrange another meeting, I told her I expected to arrive around 6.30 pm or 7 pm. Katie pointed out that she'd be working but would take a break to talk with me.

I was anxious, fearful, full of self-doubt and unsure if I was doing what was best for Katie. I was also aware that my first failed attempt to reconnect with her could understandably be interpreted as not really caring, even though nothing could be further from the truth. Still, I couldn't even begin to imagine the emotions Katie must have been dealing with.

As promised, she took a break from work and walked outside to meet with me on the footpath. To my relief she wore an enormous, beautiful smile and to my shock and amazement, she was fast becoming a woman.

We didn't hug or speak of closeness or sensitive things. I did tell her, however, that I had no intention of imposing myself on her life. We spent about thirty minutes leaning against the wall of Domino's Lismore, lightly chatting about things that weren't going to change the world, but we agreed it was good to be in each other's worlds again and that we should try to keep it up.

Looking back, the reunion was about as good as I could have expected after never really being there for her. At the same time, it fell way short of what I hoped deep down would happen. I'd allowed myself to think Katie might be so over the moon to see me that she'd drop everything and want to be part of my life. Clearly I still had a lot of work to do on 'self'.

It was the beginning of a sometimes narrow and rocky

pathway that led to new understandings of our relationship. We never gave up on the idea of being family.

Sometime during my final years in the forest – when I was trying to figure out why my life was so fundamentally unmanageable – I sketched out a simple diagram. It comprised four long horizontal lines. The top line represented 'happiness' and the bottom line represented 'depression'. When I plotted my emotional state on the chart over the course of a few months, it zig-zagged chaotically between the top line of happiness and euphoria and the base-line of depression and sadness.

The two lines I'd drawn in between those extremes, however, represented a more measured, undramatic emotional state. I figured if I could find a way to maintain my emotions between those two centre lines, my life would be much more stable. Unfortunately I was too scrambled at the time to even begin to figure out how to do that.

After the Katie disappointment, I was reminded of the diagram. I'd noticed that the happier I was, the more intense the pain when I wasn't happy. I was either elated or depressed, and I also recognised that it was a very fast trip from happiness to depression, and often a very slow journey back up.

'It's hard work being happy, and it's even harder work after I'm happy.'

I started to seriously question the wisdom of striving for happiness, and I decided I'd aim for an oscillation between the more steady inner lines of the diagram instead. To stay in the comfortable range, I had to steer away from the extreme highs. If certain behaviours were behind 'happiness', then I had to avoid them.

Meanwhile, alcohol's invisible finger kept tap, tap, tapping away. It wasn't long before I developed a new addiction to help wean the monkey off my back – sugar. I rarely went anywhere without a supply of boiled lollies, my tasty substitute for the demon drink. I was extremely fussy about which varieties passed my lips, though, as some medicated lozenges contain small traces of alcohol: something I discovered through another new obsession – reading the ingredients of every item I purchased. Being a bit of an expert in addiction, I recognised this new, all-encompassing crutch a mile off, but I accepted it for what it was.

'If I can beat the cigarettes, the alcohol and the drugs – and if I use this device of sugar to do it – I can always tackle sugar down the track.'

And tackle it I did – six years later.

I could quite easily plot a course to avoid pubs and steer clear of the drugs that were fairly available on the North Coast and Gold Coast, but I couldn't get away from cigarette smoke. A blue-grey miasma seemed to hang over the urban streets back in those days. To walk down a busy footpath was to be gassed by smokers' filthy exhaust. I'd scan for blessed jet-streams of clear air to make it from point A to point B without losing my cool.

Although I had been one for twenty-five years, all of a sudden I passionately resented cigarette smokers. I was pretty impatient and occasionally obnoxious about it, too, but I allowed myself to be a grumpy bastard:

'At least I'm not smoking. At least I'm not drinking or doing drugs.'

On a base chemical level – the receptors in my brain demanding a certain drug – I found nicotine addiction the hardest to break over the long term. The whole world annoyed the hell out of me, and while I'd given myself a free pass to be grumpy, I knew being an unpleasant narc was unsustainable. It definitely didn't fit with the new character I was trying to create for myself.

I reminded myself to look at smokers through my growing attitude of acceptance, and with the understanding that what they did was none of my business. Okay, they fouled up the air that I breathed, but so did industry, commerce, bushfires, cars, trucks and buses. All of that was out of my control, so I just let it go.

Slowly my life started to feel less like a roller-coaster and more like a series of bus rides. Instead of careening up and down, I found myself heading in the same general direction as the rest of society. Okay, I wasn't communicating with the other passengers on life's great coachline, but I was growing more content to take my place among them. Talking to people would come later.

I came to realise, too, that if I could change little parts of me one at a time, I could eventually change all of me. There were significant knock-on effects taking place, too – things that were rearranged in my favour without my addressing the problem directly.

One regrettable constant in my life had been violence. I'd been on the receiving end long before I took to self-harming in brawls, and I knew how to dispense a nasty beating, too. When I was a child, my father attacked me with abandon until I grew big enough to throttle him. In juvenile detention, explosive violence was a survival tool I used to demolish threats. As a homeless man I'd endured the misery of being bashed in my sleep.

Alcohol is a great remover and it had taken away what little capacity I had for self-protection and self-care. It hoovered up whatever crumbs of self-worth were left, too. As a consequence of locking every last person out of my world, I'd thrown the doors wide open to all manner of fighting, abuse, arguing, yelling, screaming and hating.

After my last drink, though, I was delighted to discover violence vanished entirely from my life. Like a click of the fingers! Who knew? Through abstinence, I'd begun to learn about self-protection. With drugs and alcohol no longer in the mix, I began to feel more vulnerable in situations and less inclined to expose myself to conflict of any kind.

A couple of times I inadvertently found myself in close proximity to people who were heavily intoxicated in public (that can easily happen when you're homeless). It was a surprisingly unnerving experience – like looking back in time to when I was that person, and not so long ago. I felt wary, and moved along quickly so as not to get caught in the tractor beam of trouble that pulses from people who've lost control.

That sense of self-protection and, to an extent, the invisibility of conformity became increasingly important to me. Rather than being a drunk staggering down the footpath,

I recognised that I needed to blend in more: to be 'part of' rather than 'distinct from'. Without alcohol I was changing, and I was increasingly confident that a better version of myself was taking shape.

I started giving serious thought to what a 'good man' in society might look like. What characteristics would he possess? How would he conduct himself? What would his guiding principles be? My first iteration of the ideal modern man had the traits of a knight in shining armour: valiant, brave, honest and a protector of the people. Over time I became more mature and realistic, but no less morally ambitious. I aimed to become a person who was hard working, empathetic, understanding, tolerant, generous and, above all, a family man.

Although I was carrying out significant internal renovations, my facade was weathered and peeling. To put it bluntly, I was a dishevelled, dirty, near-toothless, long-bearded and dreadlocked homeless man with a limited wardrobe of tattered smelly clothes – not exactly a suit of shining armour. I turned my attention to dressing more appropriately and found myself well placed in the Tweed Heads–Gold Coast region thanks to an abundance of op-shops. I could pick up a shirt and a pair of jeans for next to nothing. I never wasted time or money laundering them, I just threw them in the bin and bought replacements. It worked out much cheaper that way.

I put effort into personal hygiene and grooming, too, by sneaking into caravan parks to shower and comb my beard and hair. I even bought some deodorant! Once this became a habit, I started to look 'part of' even though I was still a total outsider. As a more presentable figure in the soup kitchens, I began to blend in, which allowed me to position myself more easily on the outskirts of conversation.

I was still too angry to actually speak to other human beings, but observing them and listening to them became extremely important. I'd take mental notes on what was happening in the lives of others and compare those to my own experiences, just to get a measure of where I stood in the world. A fair bit of talk in soup kitchens is framed around drug and alcohol recovery, so I paid particular attention to those little chats.

Without realising it at the time, eavesdropping in this way exercised my mind and memory. I began to recall key snippets of conversations and retain those for long periods. I realised that if something was really important to me, there was more chance of me remembering it. This fascinated me. It told me my mind could retain and locate memories – something I had struggled to do for years. This was very exciting: it gave me inspiration and something else to work on in the creation of the new Gregory.

Sharing myself with others had been a lifelong anathema and likely the main reason – on top of the slightly religious bent – that Alcoholics Anonymous was never the solution to my problems. Today, however, whenever someone seeks my advice on how to get sober, my first recommendation is for them to attend an AA meeting. It might not be for everyone, but AA has helped millions of people turn their lives around.

When I intermittently attended AA meetings during my twenties and thirties, it was all about the free coffee and biscuits. I'd go to two or three meetings and listen to what I thought was a whole lot of crap. Then, at the fourth meeting, someone would utter *just one* sentence that was mind-blowing. It could be as simple as identifying with another alcoholic. I'll never forget the bloke who said, 'Every time I drank rum, the anger inside me would explode in ways that frightened me.'

Rum was my detonator, too, so I identified with that human being and went away with something to think about.

'That guy obviously doesn't present as angry anymore. Perhaps one day I'll be able to get past my anger.'

At another meeting someone revealed, 'I had to learn to clean my teeth.' That little nugget gave me a lot of hope, too.

'Wow! I'm not the only one who has neglected myself for years!'

Still, I found the meetings largely tedious and the idea of revealing my inner struggles terrifying (spoiler alert: I never did). I'd often ask myself, 'Is it really worth investing all that time at AA for a cup of International Roast, some free Arrowroots and just one pearl of wisdom?'

When I look back today, the answer is yes. The pearls are that valuable.

Highlighting the value of past experiences, all the things I heard in meetings as a younger, angrier and broken man came back to me when I decided to quit alcohol. I pored through every file I could access in my mind in search of things I could use. Those voices from the past gave me something positive to contemplate for weeks and months. I'd pull them apart and explore all their possibilities. The wisdom of one stranger that called out from yesteryear was, 'I realise I just need to get through one day at a time.'

Bingo! Thank you for that lightbulb moment. I'd spent a lifetime haunted by my yesterdays and fearful of my tomorrows, so living one day at a time sounded like a great idea. Though again, it was so much easier said than done.

Now that I was better dressed and with my hair combed, my radar was up in the soup kitchens in the hope of catching more gold from latter-day philosophers. One morning I overheard a doozy: 'If you want to feel good, do good things,' one old fella drawled to another. 'If you want to feel bad, do bad things.'

That landed on me with a bang, and it eventually helped me integrate into society, if just a touch. A couple of weeks after I heard it, I realised I wasn't doing good things or doing bad things – I wasn't doing any things beyond simply existing and not drinking. I'd overheard people talking about a volunteer program looking after unwanted animals at the RSPCA in Tweed Heads. A day or so later I jumped on a bus and landed on the doorstep – a bit of a human stray. I won't say it suddenly made me feel good, but volunteering put me among people again, not to mention furry critters (cats, predominantly), which I understood better than I did humans. After a while I felt I had a tad more legitimacy in the community.

It was while volunteering that I realised I needed a permanent address. Securing one was a little more complicated than it first seemed. I was nowhere near ready to be set inside four walls with electricity buzzing around me. What I really needed was somewhere to satisfy bureaucracy and potential employers, as I was still applying for jobs. I reckoned a post office box would make a great first home.

Volunteering at the RSPCA and checking my PO box on a regular basis had the effect of re-stocking some of the self-worth that alcoholism had stolen from me. All of a sudden I was working (okay, voluntarily) and I had a home address (sort of). Definitely moving up in the world.

I started eating better, too, and gradually put on weight. As my memory strengthened and my mind cleared, I gained more and more perspective on how drugs and alcohol had taken over my entire being – physically, mentally and spiritually. From out of the blue an old cliché came to mind – 'Use it or lose it'. I made the decision to exercise my body, my mind and my spirit, starting pronto.

Physical exercise was difficult in the beginning, but I started by getting off the bus a few stops early and walking the rest of the way to my destination. Sometimes, if I wasn't travelling too far, I'd skip the bus entirely and hoof it instead.

To exercise my mind, I paid close attention to the world around me. In the morning I'd closely examine a flower in a park or the layout of a council garden, and in the afternoon I'd try to remember exactly what that garden looked like or how many petals were on the flower. I also worked at recalling conversations around the soup kitchens, putting faces to the stories and memorising who said what to whom.

On the spiritual front, I resolved to do a good deed for someone each day. This could be as simple as smiling at a person I really didn't have much time for, or dropping a couple of bucks on someone here and there. If they found out, it didn't count.

All of these processes slowly settled on me over many months, but it was much longer until I felt like I had gotten 'sober'. In the very early days – when I was holding on for dear life with alabaster knuckles and trying desperately not to drink – I only considered myself to be abstinent. There's a huge distinction between abstinence and sobriety. It's the difference between stopping drinking and never drinking again.

Aside from 'Are you happy?' the question I'm most often asked by people in detox and rehab centres today is: 'Is it hard to stop drinking and using drugs?'

That's a tricky one. A simple answer is, 'No, stopping is not that hard.'

People do it all the time for lots of reasons. Women stop drinking when they become pregnant, men stop if they feel they need to go on a health kick. Countless people do it every year during Dry July. *Stopping* drinking is not hard for most people, mainly because they know they can start again. *Giving up* drinking is a completely different proposition, and an infinitely more challenging one. The answer to the question then becomes, 'It's very easy to talk about giving up. It's much harder to do.'

I could probably have abstained from alcohol for years through sheer force of willpower and by separating myself from the product. The problem is that I'd still be left with all those traits and character defects: the anger, the fear, the resentment and the short temperedness – not to mention the miserable company of hurriedly buried ghosts from years gone by.

Without addressing the deeper underlying issues, without taking care of mind, body and spirit, and without creating a new character with better traits, there can be no improved quality of life. You'll always be walking on the edge. If you're scanning a newspaper, the one thing that'll stand out even larger than the full-page booze specials is that tiny little ad about alcohol in the bottom corner. That's the one that hits you right between the eyes.

'How long did it take you to get sober?' is another question that comes up a lot.

You won't be surprised that I don't have a simple answer to that. For me the acute cravings lasted about three months before they became less intense and less frequent. I still experienced moderate cravings for up to two years afterwards. Beyond that, I would only occasionally be jolted by a rogue wave of chemical desire: by then I had learned to calmly watch them roll away and disappear over the horizon.

There's one thing that I believe is an absolute in this space, though: if you remain the person who drank and used drugs, you *will* drink and use drugs again. There's no doubt that I would have, too, so I had to fundamentally change who I was: the way I thought about myself, about alcohol, about guilt, about anger, about resentment and shame. I had to rethink everything and introduce new ways of doing things. That takes time. It was about six years before I could go through a whole day without thinking about alcohol or drugs.

Today I don't even see alcohol. It's simply not a part of my world. I have friends who drink, but that's their business. I'm cognisant there is advertising and there are bottles in parks and there are pubs on corners – sometimes there's even beer and wine in my fridge – but none of it registers with me in any way. Alcohol only exists in my old life – the one that ended twenty-three years ago.

While my new life is full of opportunity, discovery, growth and achievement, there's only one thing I strive to be a perfectionist in: being sober. Ever since I left that backpack behind and started reading the ingredients on packaging, I have been hyper-vigilant about what goes into my body. Nothing else matters. Today my partner, Catherine, won't even use fermented soy sauce when she cooks for us because it contains alcohol and she knows I won't eat it.

'But it's cooked out!' she protested at first.

'I don't care,' I gently replied. 'I won't eat it.'

I won't even put a Butter Menthol in my mouth and, having survived a heroin habit in the 1980s, I give an extremely wide berth to anything that contains poppy seeds. It might sound over the top to some, but soy sauce and a little dusting of seeds on a bun are too close to the edge. I've walked on clifftops often enough to understand vertigo and I ain't for falling.

The rewards have been generous and abundant. Sobriety gave me a shot at the education I yearned for but never had, and a place in the world I could never seem to find. It has helped me understand myself and others, and it has bestowed on me peace of mind. That's the holy grail we're all looking for, isn't it? Oscillating gently between the two inner lines of contentment.

For some, peace of mind is very elusive, for others it seems unthinkable and yet for many it's just the place where they like to sit in meditation, appreciation and gratitude. I'm all about gratitude these days – it's the main course in the grand banquet of contentment. Mostly I'm grateful for where I've been and who I have become.

Sobriety's greatest gifts to me, however, have been people, beginning with myself. Alcoholism had retarded my emotions and prevented my true character from developing. Only with its banishment have I been able to discover who I am and create something more substantial than a mere knight in armour. My addictions had enslaved me to the emotions of others, which meant I had little control over who I associated with. Reversing that has been enormously rewarding. Today, every person I call a friend and everyone who is dear to me I have chosen to be there.

CHAPTER THREE
A LONELY PLANET

Contrary to what you might imagine, the loneliest times in my life did not take place during my hermit years. They didn't occur during my days as a street sleeper either. My most abject moments of loneliness arrived while I was gainfully employed, living in a house in my hometown and making positive plans for the future.

After avoiding jail for arson, I tried hard to find work and get my act together. I drifted up and down the east coast looking for seasonal jobs, but in 1988 I wound up back in Tamworth, where I found a position as a cleaner. It was a steady gig with reasonable pay and I even had enough money to take out a cheap lease on a brick house in Brisbane Street, right beside the railway tracks. It could be noisy and it wasn't much to look at, but it was neat and clean and had two good-sized bedrooms – one for me and one for Katie, who'd just turned two.

In my mind this was the beginning of something new and big. I was determined to make a go of being settled in the community and – even more importantly – building a relationship with my young daughter.

As it stood, I had one hour of supervised access to Katie each week at a community centre – a humiliating and degrading arrangement that provided zero chance of any kind of relationship, let alone a father-daughter bond. 'Access' – I hated that word. I was determined to turn the situation around by proving I was a loving, responsible and reliable parent who could take care of Katie on my own. The first step was to provide safe and appropriate accommodation where she and I could spend time together.

Coming from a background of trauma, I didn't have the firmest grasp of what 'safe and appropriate' looked like, so I had to guess at a few things and do my best. Defaulting to gender stereotypes of the day, I figured I should deck out Katie's room with lots of pink, lace and frills. I gradually populated her bed with a cast of grinning soft toys and filled the wardrobe with shoes and tiny clothes. I stocked the fridge and pantry with food and kept the place in shipshape condition. The only thing needed to complete the picture was one energetic brown-eyed toddler.

Katie's mum, Nicola, was in a raging battle with her own demons at that time and, as a result, Katie had been placed in the care of her maternal grandmother. But I never got to have Katie with me at the house in Brisbane Street. No matter how much effort I put into trying to demonstrate I was stable, reliable and worthy, I wasn't offered anything more than sixty painful and confusing minutes once a week under the scornful eye of an officious stranger.

Today I fully understand Katie's grandmother's concerns (after all, I'd firebombed a townhouse and had a reputation for being violent), but at the time I didn't think she had considered how a child could change a person's life. Granted, I may not have ended up changing enough – and I recognise a child's safety is more important than the needs of an arguably unstable parent – but back then I believed having some responsibility for Katie would have provided me with a reason to do better. At any rate, we never got to find out.

Since I'd signed a six-month lease, I was effectively imprisoned in a house that, in my mind, had become a monument to my failure as a father. The frilly pink bedroom I'd fashioned for Katie was now a mausoleum where the sorry ashes of our relationship were interred. In the small, dark hours I'd get filthy drunk and go sit in there and cry.

Those were the loneliest moments of my lonely life.

Three of my sisters happened to be living in Tamworth at the time. I reached out to them on a couple of occasions, but none of them came to visit me. I couldn't conceive of why, which only infused my intense loneliness with resentment and anger. I was in too much pain, feeling too hard done by and too full of self-pity to think about anyone else but myself. With hindsight I realise the girls were trying to work through their own emotional crises, all created in the maelstrom of our upbringing.

Most people carry friendships from childhood through adolescence, to young adulthood and into their mature years. Along the way some friends fall by the wayside, while others are added. For countless Forgotten Australians like my sisters and I, those fundamental friendships never happened. To appreciate how the State can shape a person's sense of social dislocation, removal and loneliness, it's helpful to understand who the Forgotten Australians are. Generally speaking, a Forgotten Australian is an Australian-born, non-Indigenous person who spent time in institutional out-of-home care prior to 1974. That, of course, means we are an ageing population. (Young people exiting care today are termed differently.)

In the mid-1990s, following intense lobbying, the Federal Government established a national inquiry into the Stolen Generations – 100,000-plus First Nations children who were forcibly removed from their families between 1910 and 1970. The terms of reference for that inquiry, which resulted in the landmark 1997 *Bringing Them Home* report, were very specific and related solely to Indigenous people. The airing of one national disgrace, however, shed light on another.

In 2000 the Senate launched an inquiry into the plight of people who became known as the Child Migrants. These were the 130,000 British children aged between three and fourteen who were sent to the Colonies – mostly Canada, Australia and South Africa – between 1920 and 1970 on the promise of a 'better life'. Unsurprisingly, the Child Migrants were almost always from deprived backgrounds, often taken from single mothers, and had already experienced out-of-home care in the UK. In Australia they were exposed to more 'care'. The inquiry's report, *Lost Innocents: Righting the Record*, was released in 2001 and cited 'evidence of shocking physical and sexual abuse and assault perpetrated by those charged with their day-to-day care'.

Meanwhile, as the Child Migrant investigation was winding up, another group of people began lobbying the Federal Government, essentially saying, 'What about us?' These were some of the estimated 500,000 predominantly non-Indigenous Australians who experienced the same type of brutal institutional care that was visited upon the Stolen Generations and the Child Migrants. A Senate report in 2004 outlined the abuses and called the cohort the Forgotten Australians because we had literally been forgotten in the first two reports.

I knew nothing of this when I was weeping my nights away in Katie's empty room. All I knew was that I had no relationship with my daughter and no friends. Not even the sisters who'd suffered alongside me in out-of-home care wanted to see me.

In despair and out of habit, I tried to dull the pain of loneliness with alcohol. I made awkward, drunken attempts at friendships in order to fill the hole inside me. The only place I knew where I could 'socialise' was the pub. I'd clean up other people's mess all day, then hit the local boozer around 3 pm when only a handful of barflies were hunched over schooners. By the time the place filled up after business hours, I'd be three parts gone – hardly a fit state in which to discern who might make a good friend and who might not.

The Central Hotel in Tamworth was the only pub in Australia where I refused to pick fights. I'd annexed it as a safe space in my sprawling empire of chaos: an oasis where I could relax. As late night after late night at the pub wore on, I never wanted the party in my head to end. 'Come back to my place!' I'd slur sanguinely to whichever random punter happened to be in front of me. 'We'll have a few drinks!'

It was no great surprise that those who took up the offer weren't interested in being my friend – they were just out for what they could get. Who could blame them? Desperate people attract desperate people.

Prior to moving into Brisbane Street, I'd been living in a shack near the police station in the hamlet of Bendemeer, forty kilometres up the road. It was there that I hatched an audacious plan to grow marijuana right under the nose of the law, in a small patch of bushland just behind the cop shop. It was a staggering success. As the officers went about enforcing the rules and protecting the community, my illicit crop thrived not twenty metres away. When I relocated to Tamworth to try to connect with Katie, I arrived with jars stuffed full of the harvest.

I used the drugs to cultivate relationships among the desperados who'd come over and party once the pub had closed. One such person was a woman who'd mentioned she was partial to smoking dope. When we stumbled through the door at 1 am, I started showing off and tried to fertilise our budding 'friendship' with my jars full of mischief.

'Here, take this home with ya,' I insisted, dropping a fistful of green into her open palm. 'There's plenty to go around.'

I returned the jar to the kitchen shelf alongside the salt and pepper and curry powder, and tried to have a pissed and stoned conversation with my new best pal. It turned out she had a young son, and she seemed surprised to discover I was a parent, too. Eventually she left that night with her booty of weed and the next morning I locked up and went to work, hungover as usual.

When I arrived home from the pub that night the place had been cleaned out. The drugs were gone, along with my money and meagre belongings, all the food and – most hurtful of all – Katie's clothes, toys and pretty pink bedding. I never saw that woman again, but about a year later I heard through the grapevine she'd gotten her young boy to squeeze through the doggy door at the back of the house so he could unlock the main door and let her in.

The burglary was just another degradation in a long list of indignities. To cope with it I bought vast amounts of hard liquor to drink at the house alone. An Arctic winter of depression and anxiety enveloped me, and I became too poisoned by alcohol to function at work. This only made me feel worse because I let my employers down, which meant I felt I could never face them again, and so I just stopped turning up.

It wasn't long before I fell back on tactics forged in the fires of childhood – I ran away. I cobbled together a spurious reason why I had to abandon the house and the town and move on to the next place – wherever that was. I hitchhiked out of Tamworth in the dead of night and set a heading for as far as the next ride would take me. A year or two later the lonely road led to the forest.

Loneliness is a complex and fraught psychological zone. The emotional isolation that leads to it points to a deep, driving human need for companionship and connection, if not friendship. For most of us, the craving to belong is innate.

The drivers of loneliness are highly individual, but they often include mental illnesses such as depression and anxiety. For many people loneliness springs from absent or ineffective communication skills, feelings of self-loathing, social awkwardness and fear. For others it can be a psychological symptom from being institutionalised at a young age.

For me, it was all of the above – and more. Fear, however, was a big one. I had an abiding fear of rejection, of going without, of not having somewhere to sleep, of being attacked, and a sheer terror that people might find out who I was, or at least who I thought I was: an angry, stupid, useless failure. And yet I craved attention, or visibility at the very least. I felt I had been rejected by society, because I simply wasn't acknowledged as a child, as a young adolescent or as I matured.

My seemingly congenital inability to connect caused me a lot of grief over the years. Deep-seated loneliness can lead to activities I wouldn't consider with a healthy mind: drinking spirits while sobbing in a child's empty room for months on end, for example.

Another danger of loneliness, if it's allowed to ferment for long enough, is becoming uncomfortable stepping out of it, thereby turning social isolation into a de-facto safe place. That's when loneliness becomes entrenched or 'part of who I am'.

My first experiences of intense loneliness were in the orphanage. There, the Sisters of Mercy – the cohort of nuns in charge – dealt with 'problem' children like yours truly by locking them in a dark room under the stairs. The first few times this happened to me, I encountered a loneliness more akin to full-blown terror – an absolute dread and isolation made worse by the pitch blackness. Those experiences – followed by many stints in solitary cells during my time locked up in juvenile detention – were among the primary factors that set me up for a particularly lonely life that's typical among Forgotten Australians.

While I could readily identify many of the key drivers of my life-long loneliness and point the finger here, there and everywhere, it wasn't until I got sober and tried to construct a better version of myself that I came to realise that loneliness, like acceptance, is an attitude. Once that penny dropped, I knew I ultimately had command over it.

With a sharpening mind I was able to review the central role I had played in my past and understand why I'd failed to make connections, even within my own family. As revealed to me on the park bench, *I* was the creator of much of my pain and discomfort. Accepting that also meant I could be the curator of my own contentment. It would just take some work to understand how to get there.

Alcohol, drugs and trauma had limited my capacity to see the bigger picture, which in turn primed me to experience disappointment and rejection. If I'd moved into the house in Brisbane Street with a healthier mindset, for example, I'd have been able to forge new connections for myself rather than trying to depend on broken systems (my sisters) and unhealthy relationships (the barflies).

The underlying problem was I didn't understand me. I didn't *know* me. It turned out I wasn't stupid or useless after all, I just didn't realise that I lacked the life skills necessary to be stable or provide consistency in relationships. I had never learned discernment. Coming to understand that over the past twenty years has been hugely important. Without paying attention to those deficits of character, I'd have been unable to become the person I am today – the one who knows for a fact that you can't be contented if you're lonely.

It was when I went to live in the forest that I began to understand the difference between being lonely and being alone. Loneliness is a state of emotional pain. Being alone is a state of physical removal. Loneliness can be debilitating. Being alone can be empowering.

I love being alone. It's awesome.

Living a solitary life in the forest actually helped me grow a little more comfortable with myself, at least in the early stages. I was so busy adapting to life in the wild, learning the basics of survival and exploring my magnificent new home that my mind was too occupied to accommodate the wolves and demons, too. When they came roaring back in after a year or two, my gaze turned inward.

'What's going on with me? Why am I in pain all the time? Why don't I have a place in the world?'

I'd trawl through the past and apportion blame for my woes onto a cast of absent characters – usually Mum and Dad. One night by the fire I found myself thinking about the hard life my father had lived, right up until his early death from alcoholism. He left this world a very hurt and trauma-tised person, and I pondered what a troubled boy he must have been. I concluded that his childhood probably looked a lot like mine: we were very similar in many ways and, as the saying goes, the apple never falls far from the tree.

It was while thinking about those two boys – Dad and me – that I got a sense there was a small child living inside of me and he was hurting from all the trauma and neglect. I could see that the boy required care and attention. I knew he needed a parent, but since I was so broken and barely managing to look after myself in the forest, I had no hope of connecting with him. He seemed destined to remain an orphan.

I spent thousands of nights by that fire with nothing but my thoughts for company, but as sad as my meditations became, I generally didn't feel too lonely. After all, I was out in the middle of nowhere for a reason. Now and then though, I'd find myself sitting on a moss-covered log or staring into a canyon with tears streaking down my face.

'How nice it would be for someone just to touch me or hold my hand.'

I never dared dream big about what a hug or a kiss might feel like. Just a reassuring hand on my shoulder or the soft blade of a fingertip caressing my arm would have meant the world to me.

The moment I re-entered society in 1999, however, I felt all of humanity press up close against me once again, and I was reminded of just how isolated I had become from every other human in the universe. It has never been lost on me that my epiphany arrived at the exact moment when I yearned for just one person to call a friend. So maybe *that* rates as the single loneliest moment of my life.

In recognising that loneliness hangs on a hook in the closet of attitudes, and knowing I didn't want to be lonely anymore, I resolved to do something about it. As with getting sober and drug free, addressing loneliness required concrete action. My first step? Patting cats and dogs at the RSPCA. My second step? I enrolled in a free information technology course at a community college in Tweed Heads. This not only kick-started my long dormant education, but it put me in an environment where I had to listen carefully to others.

If you're truly lonely and you want to make connections, my best advice is to go and volunteer. The RSPCA is a great place to start: you don't even have to talk to people that much, just hang out with the furry critters. The pivotal thing is to change your attitude, and be willing to change the way you think. 'Am I bold enough? Do I have the courage to change the way I'm thinking?' Willingness to keep changing is the key to growth, however, because if you're patting dogs at the RSPCA for the rest of your days, you're not really going to progress much.

As much as I love all animals, I have found that human beings deliver much better value when it comes to vanquishing loneliness. There's nothing wrong with volunteering in a soup kitchen every now and then. There's nothing wrong with volunteering in a homeless shelter either – sadly you'll find them all over the country. Even the local community centre is a good place to listen to stories and get to know people, and most have a roster for volunteers.

I found listening to others a huge help in changing my attitude of loneliness – at first in the soup kitchens and later when the IT course put me on a trajectory to study at university. Hearing what other people had to say got me out of my own head for a little while. The more I did it, the less time I spent isolated between my ears.

Even more important was understanding that the only way I'd ever get to know another human being was to listen to what they had to say. It's only by getting to know people that we begin to discern whether or not we want to make friends with them.

For the long-term lonely, the formation of friendships represents a massive turning point. Friends are like doorways into the community: once they are opened there are wonderful new pathways to be found on the other side. I was forty-seven years old before such a door opened in front of me.

My first ever adult friend was a fellow student at Southern Cross University named Lynda Lloyd. When I decided to study sociology in 2004, I had to move south from the Gold Coast to the university's Coffs Harbour campus, where a major in community development was being offered. I rented a room ten kilometres from the university and, with no public transport available, I walked it every day – rain, hail or shine.

When I mentioned this to Lynda in a brief conversation one day, she offered to give me a lift to and from the campus, since my commute was quite close to her route to the university. This gave us a lot of time to talk (mostly for me to listen) and it was in the passenger seat of Lynda's little hatchback that I realised I really liked some people!

By the time of my undergrad graduation in 2006, my new and improved attitude to loneliness was much more entrenched. I could still be very reserved at times, I still had significant mental and emotional issues to work through, but I had friends – not least Lynda and the university's charming and learned professor of social work, Richard Hil. While I have experienced growth by listening to those wonderful people and many others who are now dear and important to me, I learned a lot by watching them, too.

In some ways Richard Hil is like me when it comes to a lack of childhood friends. Although in my case this resulted from domestic trauma and institutionalisation, Richard's deficit stems from the fact that he immigrated to Australia from England and left most of his old mates behind. He has lectured in campuses all around the country, and I have noticed that whenever he moves to a new community, the first thing he does is join a tennis club. The second thing he does is start a community activist group, thereby building networks centred on common activities and interests. If defeating loneliness is developing a sense of belonging and sharing, Richard is a professor of that, too. He has taught me a lot, including discernment of what a good friend looks like.

It takes quite a while to work through the nuance and different stages of gaining a good friend. It begins as a casual acquaintance, which becomes a new acquaintance, then hopefully a friendship and over time it can develop into something truly wonderful – a reliable friend: someone you know you're important to and valued by.

A good friend will never tell you what to do or try to take something from you. A good friend won't ask you for money. A good friend cares about you, and if they say they're going to do something, it will be done. If they say they're going to meet you, they'll be there. You can have a conversation with a good friend without expectation. A good friend values the contribution you make to the relationship, just as you value theirs. If they haven't heard from you in a while, a good friend will call or text, 'Hey! How's it going?' You know you've got a good friend when you can connect after not speaking for a year and effortlessly pick up where you left it last time.

I don't experience loneliness at all these days. In fact, I haven't really felt lonely since I first committed to changing my attitude in pursuit of being a more worthwhile, more contented person. Once I commenced the journey of change, there was no going back, and it has paid rich dividends. From yearning for just one friend to tell my problems to, I now have many good friends with whom to share all my news: good, bad and boring.

From once having no social skills, I now have the ability to build a network of people I can associate with when I choose to. And I choose to a lot. From craving the faintest touch from another human, I now have a life partner who loves to hug and kiss me. There's only one problem with all this connection – I still love being alone.

Time by myself provides that opportunity for reflection and gratitude for what I have and where I am. Listening to the birds and going for a quiet walk is still very important to me. I don't miss the enforced solitude of my childhood, however, and although I often reflect on my time alone in the forest, I don't miss that either. I appreciate it because I understand where it has led me, but I would never go back.

I don't get to be alone as often as I'd like today because my commitments and responsibilities don't really allow for it. In addition to having friends, colleagues, students and acquaintances, I'm also now part of a beautiful family. Catherine and I share a house in the New South Wales town of Orange with a brood of delightful and noisy boys. Sometimes it can be hard to hear the birds. I love being a part of the chaos, though, even if it's sometimes a reminder of what was lost in my first experience as a parent. Katie is thirty-six now and a strong, smart and loving mother. I speak to her almost every day. I don't have a pink room set up for her anymore, but she has the full run of my heart.

CHAPTER FOUR
UNDER CONSTRUCTION

For a long time it seemed like the only person who believed in me was me. I had no family cheer squad, no peer support, no friends and certainly no mentor to guide me as I slowly pulled myself together. I did, however, have a gallery of grumbling naysayers happy to tear my ambitions apart.

When I passed my Certificate I in Information Technology I was so pumped and motivated that I immediately looked for other opportunities to learn. I discovered I could do a bridging course at Southport TAFE on the Gold Coast, which – if I performed well enough in it – would put me on a pathway to study at university: a mind-blowing prospect in my education-starved little world.

Nearly three years had passed since I'd left the forest, and I'd reached a point where I could say a few words to people every now and then. I could even hold a short conversation if absolutely necessary. Feeling chuffed about my exciting prospects in education, I made the mistake of mentioning the TAFE course to some of the other down-and-outers in the soup kitchens. Weathered foreheads furrowed and weary eyebrows arched.

'Mate, the only thing an education is good for is reading the measurements on a jar,' one gently spoken but perennially negative fellow opined.

Another chap pointed out that, in his experience, 'The only thing degrees are good for is reading the temperature when they shove a thermometer up your arse.'

Hmm, I hadn't thought about it quite like that before – thank goodness. It was my first and last attempt at affirmation. From then on, I ignored the musings of the amateur proctologist and his learned assistant and kept my plans to myself. Sadly, in soup kitchens and homeless shelters good people can behave like crabs in a bucket: as soon as anyone tries to climb out, half a dozen claws reach up and methodically drag them back in.

Much of this behaviour stems from cynicism fuelled by ignorance. Some of it is resentment cut with a bit of self-pity, too. A lot of the guys who bagged out my goals no doubt cultivated dreams of their own from time to time but, for whatever reason, struggled to make them come true. Furthermore, since I hardly spoke, they didn't know the first thing about me, so it was difficult for them to connect and put forward constructive comments.

As a loner, I generally looked for encouragement and inspiration elsewhere anyway. I'd become an avid collector of clichés, old sayings, truisms and memes. I'd pluck them out of old songs, harvest them from overheard conversations and even swipe them from graffitied walls. One of my favourites appeared on a sign outside a Coolangatta church: 'Now is the greatest gift of all. That's why they call it The Present.'

I loved that and tried to take it to heart. In fact, it's a gift that keeps on giving today.

Undaunted by pessimistic mutterings in the soup kitchens, my yearning for a better life grew stronger. In accepting that there would always be critics, I found comfort in the old saying, 'You can't please all of the people all of the time.' Had I tried, I'd have careened all over the place and been unable to make a single decision. Since I was the sole person in my corner, I only needed to please me.

I doggedly applied myself to my endless challenges day in, day out. Not that you'd know by looking at me. In the soup kitchens I looked like any other sitting duck with a haunted expression, but below the surface I was paddling furiously to make headway. Since my mouth was almost always shut, I often thought I might benefit from a T-shirt printed with a slogan to do the talking for me: 'No access for the next three years. Major construction in progress.'

In addition to the capital works already underway (the reversal of a great river of alcohol and the building of psychological bridges to help me return to society), there were countless potholes, blocked roads and flooded byways that needed my attention. Working through them one at a time gradually helped smooth the path forward.

After the epiphany on the park bench, I had started with the premise that I knew what *wasn't* good for me. In the process of eliminating those elements from my life, I decided I could try to work with whatever was left. If it benefited me, great. If it didn't, then I'd get rid of it too.

Ditching my forest attire and paying attention to personal hygiene had already created a gestational bump in my self-esteem. While sprucing up my outsides hadn't been overly challenging, it opened the door to some more confronting internal rehabilitation. For example, I knew I hadn't looked anybody in the face, let alone their eyes, for decades – if ever.

This regrettable character flaw had been drilled into me in the boys' homes. Inmates were instructed not to look at the guards or even at each other. No one needed a reminder to avoid meeting my eyes: I was marked out as the resident 'psycho' who was likely to smash your face in at the faintest sideways glance. The life lesson we all learned in juvenile jail, however, was clear and simple: 'You are not worthy of looking at your betters.'

Shame is a sharp blade that can be used to cut individuals and vulnerable groups from the cloth of society. Weaving oneself back in can take a long time, as I was finding out. In the orphanage and the boys' homes, and even in my own family, I was repeatedly told I would never amount to anything. In the juvenile justice system, I was informed I had a low IQ that made it impossible for me to perform as well as the other inmates, and I was subjected to isolation in order to make me feel even worse. As soon as I was released from the solitary confinement, those with power talked down to me in front of other boys and encouraged them to see me as something lower, too. I was forced to scrub footpaths or stand on a chalked cross while the other boys played because I was less.

By the time I went to live in the forest fifteen years later, I was clothed in immense shame. It was all I knew: the shame of not being the person I should have been, the shame of not keeping my word, of breaking promises, of being drunk all the time, of being a failure and the great shame of not having a place to live. How do you even begin to come back from that?

A couple of years ago I was asked to contribute some thoughts on the travails of homelessness for a book about the hardship of street sleeping. I wrote:

> '*Most Australians find it hard to look at a homeless person. They prefer to stare straight ahead and pretend that the hungry, damaged and lonely human being in their peripheral vision simply doesn't exist. Apparently it's just easier that way. If refusing to even make eye contact with a homeless person is hardwired in the masses, then talking to them and listening to their stories is out of the question.*'

I was making two points: first, the creation of shame usually takes two and, second, the power to vanquish it is literally in the eye of the beholder.

In some cultures, looking people in the eye is inappropriate, but in Australia it's what we do to demonstrate mutual recognition and respect. I was sitting in a soup kitchen one day, pondering ways to throw off the cloak of shame, when a song lyric came to mind from all the way back in 1964: Val Doonican's 'Walk Tall', which celebrated the value of standing up straight and looking the world right in the eye.

It was sad to think that I'd walked out of the institutions at age nineteen to make my way in the world with my eyes cast down. No wonder I crashed clumsily through life, smashed into relationships, got completely lost and hurt myself along the way. Even during the final few years alone in the forest, I had hung my head low. I hadn't seen a sunrise or the majestic flare of the Milky Way in a long time. I had simply stopped looking at the horizon, let alone to the celestial heavens.

I certainly knew what 'down' looked like, though: dirt, rocks, my boots, cigarette butts, empty bottles and a lapful of sorrows. But now with a clear mind, combed beard and brand-new second-hand clothes, I managed to muster just enough nerve to lift my chin and start looking up.

It had a huge impact, particularly in concert with sobriety. Looking up revealed that the dawn was as beautiful as ever, that sunlight bathed the planet with a warmth and equity that bonded my fortunes to those of all living things. I made a point of watching the sunrise and looking at people when I passed them. Where once I saw humans as goblins, trolls and demons – the perpetrators of all the horror in my world – I began to see elves, fairies and a sprinkling of hobbits in the mix. They appeared in many guises: a friendly and helpful tutor at TAFE, a chatty fellow student, and a selfless stranger who helped me find my first home in nearly seventeen years.

Although I was a constant source of food for the mosquitoes, dune life on the Gold Coast had been bearable – not only due to the temperate climate but because any kind of existence is more orderly when you're sober. My camp remained extremely small and tidy, and never once attracted the attention of council rangers.

When I left the forest, it occurred to me that the last time I'd had a roof over my head was during my miserable stint in Brisbane Street, Tamworth, in 1987. As my stack of textbooks and folders grew in the dunes on the Gold Coast, along with my workload for the bridging course at Southport TAFE, I needed to get myself out of the elements and into secure accommodation in order to live and study. Making that giant leap was much harder than I thought. I tried and failed multiple times.

I was sitting on a suburban park bench on the Gold Coast one afternoon in 2003, weeping with frustration at my inability to rent a place, when a woman in a floral dress stopped and asked me what was wrong. Uncharacteristically, I poured my heart out to her. I explained that I'd been homeless for years and how I'd asked a student counsellor at TAFE for help in finding a place to live but he'd brushed me off with, 'Just go to a real estate agent and they'll sort you out!'

The problem was I'd become so unsocialised I didn't know how to do the basics, like talk to a realtor or organise a lease. The woman listened sympathetically as my woes and frustrations spilled out. When I fell silent, she helped me to my feet and walked with me to a nearby suburban real estate agent. Within a couple of days, she had helped me get a lease and move into a one-bedroom ground floor unit in the shade of monolithic Gold Coast high rises. Finally, I was secure. I even had the company of a stray cat that had decided to move in, too.

Although I'd felt a lot of shame and stigma around not having a home, it was unrealistic to think my lifelong issues would be easily addressed by a roof and four walls. In a matter of weeks, I became claustrophobic, anxious and depressed in my new abode. It was clear I wasn't ready for that type of living yet – if ever.

The decision to abandon the flat was a reflection of my new modus operandi:

'If it doesn't work, ditch it.'

My only regret was leaving the cat behind.

In late 2003, to my complete amazement, I passed the Special Tertiary Admissions Test at Southport TAFE with an excellent mark – high enough to unlock the gates to university. I decided to study sociology at Southern Cross University, which saw me move from the dunes at Tweed Heads closer to the Coffs Harbour campus in 2004, where I made a second attempt at living in a flat. This one, near my daily rendezvous with Lynda Lloyd, was quieter and brighter than the place on the Gold Coast, and I was more easily able to focus on my studies.

I had initially chosen to study sociology in order to understand why society and I had long seemed to have a mutual loathing of each other. Moving to Coffs Harbour was a pivotal point in my new life, not just from an academic point of view – it signalled the end of decades of homelessness. Once I moved into that flat, I never slept rough again.

I'm often asked how I managed to afford higher education, given I had no savings or income beyond a disability support pension. Well, like all university students in Australia, I qualified for the Higher Education Contribution Scheme (HECS), which meant I didn't have to start repaying the cost of my fees until I commenced working.

As part of my undergraduate degree, I was invited to do an Honours year. My thesis, 'I'd Like to Tell You a Story but I'm Not Sure if I Can', explored the experiences of people who had been abused in the same Catholic orphanage where I had suffered as a child. I was privileged to earn first-class Honours for that work, which led to me being offered an Australian Postgraduate Award Scholarship to do a PhD.

The stipendiary scholarship meant I was actually paid to do my research and study. I was also offered work at Southern Cross University to bolster my academic skills by tutoring students and marking exams. So that's how I paid for my education, in money terms anyway. The rest was done with hard graft and dedication. It had its moments, but I had promised myself I would be the best person I could. The man I had in mind was no longer a knight of the realm, but he was no longer a quitter either.

In February 2012 I had saved enough money to take out a mortgage on a 25-acre plot at Lanitza, a pleasant rural locale between Coffs Harbour and Grafton. I erected a sturdy and liveable steel shed, built a chook pen, put in a water tank and wired some solar panels to a battery set-up. It is my off-grid sanctuary far from the crowds and murmuring power lines. I still have that property, and I still rent the unit in Coffs Harbour, too. Today, however, my home – physical, spiritual and emotional – is in Orange with Catherine and the boys.

The journey back from chronic homelessness had been long and confounding, but the very first step had been to look up. Sometimes when I think about it today my mind will fill with the strains of 'Amazing Grace':

> *'I once was lost, but now I'm found*
> *Was blind but now I see.'*

Had I not raised my gaze to meet that of the guardian angel in the floral dress, I might not have ended up quite where I am today.

In opening my eyes and my mind to society for the first time, it dawned on me that I don't so much *see* ugly, I hear it instead. I began to realise that when you listen to people, they tell you who they are, and you'd do well to believe them.

That penny dropped with a particularly discordant clatter one day when I observed an elegant, well-dressed and extremely attractive fellow student in a hallway at Southport TAFE. Since she was so outwardly beautiful, I couldn't help but steal a couple of glances at her, but when she opened her mouth to speak, I had to look away. Seemingly out of nowhere, she exploded at a couple of young students who were sitting on the floor, partially blocking the passageway.

'Move!' she bellowed. 'This is where people walk. It's a fucking hallway, not a sitting room. What right do you have to be sitting on the floor, you pieces of shit? How fucking dare you? People like you make me sick.'

In that moment, the young woman became the ugliest human being I'd encountered in a long time.

It made me think about how ugly I must have come across – or at least sounded – for much of my life. My obnoxiousness, arrogance and my serrated tongue had made sure of that. Even more reason for me to change. It was a relief to discover, however, that the vast majority of people are beautiful. We might not all be aesthetically perfect but, for the most part, humans are very decent and kind in the things they do and say.

I don't think I smiled for years after coming out of the forest. I believe the first time I exercised those particular muscles in my new life was in Coffs Harbour, probably in response to something Lynda Lloyd said as we drove to uni together. A smile is an invitation for people to keep talking to you. I found the more I smiled, the more I had to say, too.

I work a lot with homeless people these days – folks who have faced hard times in life that aren't getting much better. I do a lot of listening in that role, but I almost always look for an opportunity to try to make them smile. If I can do that, I've opened the gateway. All it takes is one tiny smile and that gives me permission to keep talking and explore their stories a little more: where they come from, what they're going through and where they hope to get to one day. There are some fascinating and beautiful souls sheltering behind stony faces.

The glamazon hall monitor with the vicious streak had also reminded me to never judge a book by its cover. As a vagrant, I'd been badly misread by that measure for decades. Even today, my long hair and beard attract a few disapproving looks and I can see people forming an opinion of me, especially when I wear my hippie pants. What they'll never know is that I have worked hard to improve myself for nearly a quarter of a century. I'll never be perfect, but I know I'm no longer ugly.

Accordingly, today I make no assessment of people whatsoever until they start to talk. Only then can I begin to understand their views and observe how they treat others. I can only hope people take the same approach with me. I have become very particular about choosing the right words, and I always weigh the impression I want to make. I alone have control over what I say. I know my words have the power to influence: they can hurt people, and they can make people sad or angry or happy, so I need to be aware of what I say, understand it and care about it. That's part of the reason I swore off swearing.

As out of control as my father was, I never once heard him use a curse word. Dad always said, 'People who swear are only highlighting their limited vocabulary.' (When I mentioned this to my good friend Craig Henderson, the writer who helped me pen my memoir, he said with a wink, 'That's fucking bullshit, mate!')

I take Craig's point – one can have a good vocabulary and still swear – but I had decided my voice would be uncontaminated by profanity. Although I'd tried to follow Dad's example throughout my life, I was guilty of dropping the odd F-bomb in times of frustration, dismay and rage. In the soup kitchens of my healing, however, I heard so much obscene language it started to wear pretty darned thin. There were a couple of guys I'd overhear who could swear non-stop for a full minute without repeating themselves.

I'm no saint and I still let slip the occasional low-level oath, but the marquee words of offence – the barrage of Fs and Cs you hear more and more these days – no longer pass my lips. I don't judge those who swear: after all, we are products of our environment, our upbringing and our tribes. I'd just rather do without it, that's all.

After I discovered my radar for verbal ugliness and cleaned up my own language, however, I became acutely aware of how perilous my interactions with other people could be. Even today I know I can come across as artless and inappropriate. Although my intent is never to be rude or cruel, and even though I've worked hard to get my anger under control, I know I can unwittingly present as, well, just a bit . . . odd. Trauma and isolation rendered me socially inept and extremely uncomfortable when it came to conversation. While that has improved over the past ten years or so, I'm still just as likely to say something awkward or jarring without realising it.

I was in a shop not so long ago and when the lady serving me asked how my day was going, I replied, 'Bearing up under the stress of modern day living.' Normally I respond to such inquiries with 'Fine, thanks' or 'Good, thanks', but for some reason I was chatty – maybe because she had a nice smile.

As she handed me my change, another woman joined her

behind the counter. 'Is that your mum?' I asked before I had time to realise it was a weird thing to say.

'No,' she said evenly. Her sunny tone had disappeared and so had the smile. I followed up with another odd utterance: 'Sorry! I didn't think!' before hurrying out of the shop.

By the time I started at university I decided it was important, if I felt like I'd said something inappropriate or offended someone, to seek them out and clarify what I'd meant as soon as possible. It was important to me that I explained I had no ill intentions. My mantra for that was:

'Don't let indiscretion become an infection.'

I already had enough actual malaises to deal with.

Disposing of intoxicants and pollutants had done me a great deal of good, but no amount of clean living was going to erase the fact that I had trashed my body for a long time. There was a price to pay. During my forest years I became so malnourished my teeth literally rotted away in my skull. When I returned to society, only a few remained. For the first time since my teenage years, I sought an appointment with a dentist, who set about rebuilding my dilapidated mouth. This did wonders for my dignity, much more than running a comb through my hair.

With a new grille of false teeth, I continued to tinker under the hood. While there was much work to do mentally, other physical ailments kept popping up. The most serious by far was the diagnosis I received in 2006 for hepatitis C – a deadly time bomb that had been silently ticking away ever since I used dirty needles during my heroin days. Thankfully a treatment had been developed for the sub-type genome that affected me and I was cured. The episode underscored the importance of treating my body more like a temple than a dead horse, particularly since I was into my middle age.

While none of us can rival Benjamin Button, today – with my seventieth birthday coming into view – I am as physically vital as I was before I entered the forest at thirty-five. I live a clean life. I am a vegetarian. I exercise and I pace myself in what has become a fairly hectic schedule of work, advocacy and family. I am living proof that however badly you have treated yourself, it's never too late to turn things around.

By the time I was neck deep in my PhD thesis ('Nobody's Children: An Exploration into Adults Who Experienced Institutional Care'), my way of thinking, my outlook on life and my understanding of the human condition had changed significantly. This time of awakening would see some relationships I'd formed fall away and others blossom. Every relationship I forged during the years of resurrection were important to me and they remain so today. Even the ones that didn't last were beautiful gifts that presented me with opportunities to learn and develop.

By 2016, when my doctorate was conferred, I needed to be on my own. Before I embarked on my PhD, Southern Cross University had insisted I see a psychologist out of a concern that I might experience vicarious trauma. This is how I came to meet the wonderful Christina North, who remains my friend – and sometimes my shrink, too. Although I wasn't retraumatised by my PhD research, I did need time to recover, reflect and re-evaluate who I was becoming, and ponder the direction in life I wanted to go.

I had been marking and grading assignments at Southern Cross University and was offered work as a casual lecturer at the Coffs Harbour campus. It had been sixteen years since my last drink or drug, and my modest new career in academia began to sit more easily on my shoulders.

I was just settling into this new existence when I was invited to do an interview on the popular ABC Radio program *Conversations* with Richard Fidler. Word about my unusual path to a doctorate had got around the university and eventually made its way to the national broadcaster. The interview with Richard altered the course of my life. By the time I got home from the ABC studio in Brisbane, I was deluged with offers to write a book. When *Out of the Forest* was published in 2018, life shifted gears again as my story hit the national media.

I was gobsmacked to see myself featured on ABC TV's *Australian Story*, not once but twice. Millions of people have watched the episodes. In 2021 I delivered a TEDx Talk in Byron Bay in the hope that my story might help even one other person dealing with homelessness and trauma. At the time of publication, it had clocked more than one million views on YouTube.

After wasting half of my life, I have gone from being an unsmiling anti-social recluse who struggled to communicate with a shopkeeper to a public speaker, an advocate and leader in my field. It's been a very challenging journey. I am grateful for the doors that have opened in front of me, and particularly that I now have a platform from where I can shine a light on and work to address homelessness, abuse, neglect and trauma among some of the most vulnerable people in society.

One of the not-so-great aspects of having a public profile, however, is the mild degree of celebrity that has come with it. I know I'm not exactly John, Paul, George or Ringo, but now and then I'll get pulled aside by someone who'll say, 'Oh, I remember you – you were on *Australian Story*!' or 'I heard you on Richard Fidler's show!' or 'Hey man, I read your book!'

That can be fairly uncomfortable for me. Not that anyone has been negative or offensive: people are always very kind and usually they seem excited to meet me, which, of course, I find bizarre. As strong as my impulse is to crawl into the nearest hole, I recognise that it's a moment for them and I try really hard not to deflate it. Okay, I might feel awkward for a minute or two, but not as bad as we'd both feel if I turned away when they said, 'Hey man, I read your book . . .'

Far better to say, 'Hello. Yes, I'm Gregory. Thank you. How do you do?'

After all, these moments give me a wonderful opportunity to continue the spiritual callisthenics I undertook in my early days off the park bench: 'Do something kind for a stranger.'

In today's world, where we all have the opportunity to broadcast our opinions on social media, it's not uncommon that I'm critiqued, too. While it's never said to my face, plenty of people have stated a belief online that by leaving the forest and re-joining society I have sold out: I have come back to the mothership of the corporatocracy to be brainwashed and programmed to meet societal expectations.

I imagine that perspective comes from the romantic notion that the forest was all bliss and enlightenment. It wasn't – especially after the first few years had passed by. The proof of this is in the medical records. When I came out of the forest, I was emaciated, weighing around half of what I do today. I couldn't stand up straight and my mind was scrambled, too. Hardly romantic stuff. There's nothing windswept and interesting about reaching into your mouth with filthy fingers and ripping your teeth out. There's nothing free-spirited or edgy about chronic gastroenteritis caused by drinking putrid moonshine made with stagnant creek water.

As for being brainwashed, I'd argue that my healing has taught me freedom of thought instead. I have had to develop my own critical thinking and critical analysis to enable my forward movement. If somebody tells me something new, I generally question it. I know I have an inquiring mind, which is how I know degrees are not only useful on rectal thermometers.

For all the progress, the good thoughts, the noble aims, the goals met and the acceptance received, I still had an extremely hard time reconciling with my past. Making peace with who I'd been and the terrible things I'd done to others took me years. Indeed, it continues today.

CHAPTER FIVE

FORGIVENESS IS FOR GIVING

If life is a highway, I'd spent the first forty-five years hurtling along in the battered station wagon of my soul, going in the wrong direction. I'd hung onto the wheel with one hand and tossed the receipts for every mistake I'd ever made into the back seat, out of sight and out of mind. Now that I'd jumped on the brakes, though, all that crap landed back in my lap where I had no choice but to deal with it if I wanted to be free from emotional turmoil. One of the first items on the agenda was the hurt I had caused my five little sisters.

I had once taken my role as their big brother very seriously. I worried about them and tried to watch over them when our parents were on the rampage. I'd often put myself between them and a kick or a slap from Dad or an old-fashioned whipping with the jug cord from Mum. But after our parents abandoned us to the orphanage, I lost my power as protector. I couldn't shield the girls or shape their fortunes any more than I could my own. Catholic dogma, institutional abuse and gender separation drove a wedge between us. From then on I was little more than a fleeting presence in their lives as mine fell to pieces.

The last time I spoke to any of the girls was in late 1989, not long before I went to live in the forest in Goonengerry. I'd called Glenda, the eldest of the five, from a phone booth one stormy afternoon in Brisbane. Even today, the only words I recall from that conversation are, 'You know, Gregory, you're a very intelligent man but you have absolutely no common sense.'

I slammed the phone down and from that moment on I didn't speak to Glenda, or any other members of our family. I thought about my sisters a lot during my lost years, as I replayed Mum and Dad's greatest hits in my mind, but it never prompted a phone call or a letter, let alone a visit. Although in my immaturity I was a resentful and judgemental person, deep down I always knew there were things I had said and done that my sisters deserved an apology for, and now the receipt was sitting in my lap.

It arrived during my first year at university, when studying sociology started to help me articulate the personal transformation I was going through, and to understand what had happened to all of us as children. Yes, there was a lot to be said for malfunctioning systems and the failings of others in our wretched lives, but as my perspective changed and my thinking matured, I felt the full weight of remorse for the harmful decisions I'd made. With each passing day I felt compelled to find the girls and say sorry to them.

Nice idea, huge challenge. The only one I vaguely knew the whereabouts of was Glenda. By then I had acquired a mobile – an old brick of an Ericsson 'dumb phone' – and although I didn't have her contact number or address, I recalled that she had moved to Sydney. The good news was her surname was no longer Smith; the bad news was it was almost as common. This was in the days before Facebook, so I found myself a copy of the Sydney *White Pages* and got to work.

After a day or so I'd narrowed the search for Glenda to six likely phone numbers. It took me a while to build up the courage, and I had a queasy feeling in my gut, but eventually I started cold-calling the shortlist. When I dialled the second number, I immediately recognised the lady who said, 'Hello?'

After one last moment of hesitation I quietly said, 'Glenda, it's Gregory.'

'We thought you were dead somewhere!' my long-lost sister blurted out, her trembling voice cut with shock and indignation.

I told her I was quite okay and hadn't used drugs or alcohol for a couple of years. I didn't say too much else about that as I was feeling a bit shocked, too. These were baby steps. I explained that I was having a go at making a better life, and to her credit, Glenda listened to what I had to say. I apologised for the long time between calls and for hanging up on her fourteen years earlier.

There were some long silences and I could tell she was seriously rattled. I didn't want to upset her any more, so I kept the call fairly short. 'Glenda,' I said, 'would it be okay with you if I called you again, once you've had time to absorb this?'

To my relief she agreed, and we arranged for a phone call the following week, which also gave me time to consider what I was going to say and how I'd say it. When I phoned her back a few days later, we exchanged the standard salutations and I asked her if it would be okay if I spoke freely.

'By all means,' Glenda consented.

Over the next little while, I spoke of my many regrets for my past transgressions and failures: for not being the best brother I could be, for not being around and for leaving her wondering if I was dead or alive. I apologised without qualification and without asking for anything in return.

When I finished, Glenda acknowledged what I'd said and told me she'd spoken to our other sisters. 'They're angry, Gregory,' she said. 'I very much doubt they'll want to speak to you.'

I asked Glenda for their addresses anyway, gave her my mobile number and said she could pass it on to the others if she wished. 'If you ever want to call, I will always answer or phone you back. You have my word, Glenda,' I said.

A week later she rang and thanked me for the previous chat. With that we started to develop a relationship. Around twelve months later, she trusted me enough to let me visit her at home in Sydney. Not so the other girls. It would be years before I managed to speak to all of them.

Contacting Glenda without any warning had been fraught enough, so, knowing the others were mightily displeased with me, I knew I would have to tread very gently.

There was no way I could arrive on their doorsteps and upend a bin full of my shame on them. Not even baby steps were going to cut it: I would have to be content to crawl.

On Christmas Day 2004, I was volunteering at a soup kitchen when my phone rang. 'It's your sister Wendy,' a gruff voice at the other end said. 'I heard you got off the drink . . .'

So began the process of apologising to Wendy and, eventually, helping her overcome her own struggle with alcohol. We formed a very close and meaningful relationship, which in time became a pathway to reconnections with my three other sisters.

The entire exercise had been built on the foundation of what they needed and deserved from me, not the other way around. I didn't covet their forgiveness: I only wanted to do what was honourable and decent, and if I found some relief from my guilt and shame in the process, so be it. My aim had been simple: turn up, be present and listen to them. I resolved to have no agenda other than to acknowledge my wrongdoings and offer my apologies. I would make no demands on them. I would have no expectations. If they wanted to say something, I would shut my mouth, look at them and let them speak without interruption. When they'd finished – unless they invited me to respond – I would humbly acknowledge their feelings and words.

Glenda hadn't been kidding: my sisters had been absolutely furious with me and I wasn't surprised to discover their main and uniting grievance was that I had vanished from the face of the earth. All of them had worried that I had died long ago – an open-ended anguish endured by the families of all missing persons. Over the years they slowly allowed me the space to say my piece. It was quite a thing to sit across a table from someone who had wept over my early death, simply because I'd been too selfish to send up even the faintest smoke signal.

Comprehending the depth of their suffering brought me to my knees. I didn't argue, I didn't qualify points or make any excuses. I acknowledged what they said and how they felt, and I apologised for the pain I had caused them. While being accountable to my sisters had never been about seeking forgiveness, they all gave it to me – a benevolence that lightened the load of my remorse and helped change my life. Today we are the very best of friends.

The holes I'd kicked in my memory had a particularly unsettling consequence during my first few years back in the world: extreme paranoia. Without drugs and alcohol to blur the lines of reality, I found myself constantly assessing people, genuinely concerned they might be someone I'd bashed, insulted or offended in the past.

'What if someone recognises me, sneaks up and cracks me across the back of the skull?'

The more clarity of thought I achieved, the worse the paranoia became. It was clear that if I wanted to live a life free of shame and remorse – and indeed the spectre of getting jumped – I'd have to act.

In the wake of making myself accountable to Glenda I decided that – if I could find them – I would apologise to every person I had ever wronged. There was a cast of thousands, including countless strangers I'd assaulted or abused who I'd likely never see again. However, there were plenty of people I *did* know. Some of the worst slights dated back twenty and thirty years.

One of the receipts I held was for a bikie I'd headbutted in the face at the Imperial Hotel in Tamworth in 1988. Naturally, that had led to some measure of enmity between us. A few days after that sickening assault, he spotted me outside the house I was renting in Brisbane Street and attacked me. In the melee, I managed to take a hold of his thumb between my teeth. His attempted retribution for the bar room headbutt disappeared in terrible howls of agony and we'd left it at that.

It had happened so long ago that I wasn't expecting any kind of reprisal, but I just couldn't stop feeling sorry about it. I knew the bikie's name, but I had no idea where he lived. Fortunately I knew who his mum was, and a quick search of the trusty *White Pages* revealed she still lived in Tamworth.

I wrote to her, enclosing a stamped letter that I'd written to her son, and asked her if she'd mind posting it to him on my behalf. I never really expected it to be delivered but I'd promised myself I would make every effort to be accountable to *everyone*. About a month later I received a letter with an address in northern New South Wales handwritten on the back.

'If you're ever in Kyogle, drop in and say g'day!' my old biffing buddy had offered.

It caught me off guard. *Ah okay, here we go. How's this going to unfold?*

There was only one way to find out. A week later I was on my way to Kyogle. I was extremely nervous as I followed the winding, tree-lined roads that trace the rivers of the north coast.

'What if it's an ambush?'
'What if he headbutts me?'

'What if he doesn't accept my apology?'
'Remember, this is not about you. This is not about you.'

My heart was a thundering timpani as I knocked on the flimsy fly-screen door. A large tattooed man quickly filled the entrance and peered intently through my enormous beard and the mists of time. 'Orgh, g'day, ya old bastard!' he said, chuckling and smiling widely when he recognised the face that had once tried to chew his thumb off. 'How the hell are ya, mate? Come in and have a beer!'

'Sorry, I don't drink,' I said. 'But I'd love to come in. It's good to see ya too.'

He fixed us each a cup of tea and as we sat down, I got straight to the point. 'Look, I just wanted to come here and apologise unconditionally for everything I did to you.'

We looked at each other for a few silent seconds and I felt like we were scared and confused little kids stuffed inside the bodies of middle-aged men.

'Listen mate,' he finally said, smiling again, 'it was just as much my fault as it was yours. We were both young, we were both a bit wild and probably pissed to the eyeballs, too.'

I couldn't argue with any of it, even if I'd wanted to. When I left that afternoon, we shook hands and he patted me on the shoulder. 'Come back any time,' he said. 'Just let me know and I'll put the jug on.'

I have approached in the order of twenty people over the years and I'm not sure I'm finished yet. One encounter that took nearly fifteen years to eventuate was with a man who I was at once deeply ashamed and highly motivated to meet.

Putting aside the challenges of my upbringing, there were legitimate reasons why I'd been locked up as a teenager. To bankroll my regular efforts to run away from home and the orphanage – which sometimes saw me make it as far as Queensland before being rounded up and sent back – I'd turned to petty crime and burglary. During one late night break-and-enter in Tamworth, I was nabbed red-handed by the homeowner. I was arrested, charged, made a Ward of the State and imprisoned for twelve months.

Violating the sanctity of that man's home was one of the most shameful acts of my life. I had to swallow my pride to write about it in *Out of the Forest* in 2018, which is how I came to be sitting across from him a year later.

I remembered his surname was Mitchell, but I knew nothing about him beyond that, and I'd long suspected he'd passed away. After my book was released – and aided by social media – I suddenly found myself being contacted by quite a few people from my childhood. I started corresponding with a former classmate, and in 2019 we arranged to meet up. It seemed her sole purpose in life was to know absolutely everybody in Tamworth. When I mentioned my regret about the attempted burglary one day, she chirped brightly, 'I know that person!'

'Would you be able to introduce me?' I asked in a flash. 'Would you ask him if he'd be willing to meet with me?'

A few months later I was sitting in Mr Mitchell's house in Tamworth (not the scene of the crime, he'd moved), cradling another cup of peace tea. Not only had I tried to rob him when I was seventeen, but my friend informed me that Mr Mitchell happened to be an ex-cop. I had no idea what to expect from the man.

'I know what I did was wrong and that it hurt you and your family,' I began quietly. 'Everyone has the right to feel safe in their own home. I humbly apologise to you and want you to know I'm working very hard to change.'

I was trembling, just as teenage Gregory had been as the stony-faced magistrate handed down his sentence in 1973, but Mr Mitchell's response was quite extraordinary.

'That's all done and dusted, son,' he said softly, leaning forward on his kitchen table. 'You were just a kid and you paid dearly for it. You've obviously learned a lot from that, too, I imagine.'

I nodded and told him I had, and how I was still learning every single day. 'Often from moments like this and people like you.'

Although it was an unplanned by-product of atonement, I received forgiveness from every single person I apologised to. It had a massive impact on my wellbeing and became a central plank in the development of my new self. In making amends where I could, I not only shed the excess weight of guilt and remorse, but I established in myself the principle that I am true to my word. I *was* sorry, I meant it, and I made sure I followed through. Every. Single. Time. No mucking around.

Just like physical discomfort, our painful emotions exist for a reason. If you stick your hand in a fire, your body tells you pretty quickly to pull it back out. If you're experiencing regret, guilt, shame or remorse, that's your mind telling you there's a problem and you need to fix it, pronto.

I reject the old adage that 'time heals all wounds', because the mental injuries from remorse and shame do not fade with each lap around the sun. In fact, time compounds them. Tragically, I know of people who have died by suicide because of their inability to live with the accumulation of guilt and regret. Action is the only thing I know of that can turn those emotions around. Ol' mate in the soup kitchen knew it, I know it and so do you: 'If you want to feel bad, do bad things. If you want to feel good, do good things.'

It's important to understand, however, there will always be loose ends. You can't always tie a pretty bow on the past. Some people will have died, some will have moved on, others will be lost in the ether and some won't want to hear from you. Once again, what's crucial is the *willingness* to be accountable whenever the opportunity presents itself and being prepared to take the time to do it.

There was no way I was going to deal with my past wrongs all at once. It was far too big a task, so I just faced one person at a time. Now and then the universe stepped in and gave me a little push, too, and I had to go digging through all the receipts to figure out what it was telling me. One such curve ball was a massive debt I owed to all Australians.

Although I'd been homeless for many years and only began my career in academia in 2008, I had worked for much of my life. I got my first job sweeping floors in a Tamworth engineering workshop at fourteen and nine months – the age at which Dad could legally pull me out of school and send me to work to help pay the household bills (I was living back at home at the time, after sixteen months in the orphanage).

I held a handful of slightly less menial positions over the years that followed, but for the most part I never rose above the station of a shop floor shit-kicker.

The last job where I'd paid tax on my earnings was cleaning floors and making car suspension springs at a factory in Sydney when I was twenty-five. Every position after that was a cash-in-hand affair. I was itinerant, too, constantly chasing happiness, or at least a semblance of a fresh start, in every new town. I'd manage to keep a job for a few weeks or months and then disappear into the next misadventure right up and down the eastern seaboard. That went on for ten years, during which time I never gave the government a whiff of my hard-earned. I drank it, shot it up and smoked it all instead. Now my serial tax-avoidance began to gnaw at me and I wanted to fix it – particularly since the taxpayers of Australia were funding my disability support pension.

I made an appointment with the Australian Taxation Office at their premises in Brisbane. I was extremely apprehensive about it all: I knew tax avoidance was a serious offence and people sometimes went to jail for it. Although I tried not to, I conjured frightening visions of what might happen next. While my mind filled with worst-case scenarios involving handcuffs and holding cells as I shuffled inside the large office block in the Queensland capital, I felt sure I was doing the right thing.

No sooner had I sat down opposite a young man in a collar and tie than I confessed to financial crimes against the Commonwealth. 'I've been a naughty boy,' I began sheepishly. 'I haven't paid any taxes for a very, very long time.'

The fresh-faced taxman had my file open on his computer and I imagined the last transaction tied to my tax file number related to the Sydney car spring factory in 1982. 'So, you've been earning income elsewhere and not paying tax on that, is that what you're telling me?' he asked.

'Guilty as charged,' I replied, my shoulders drooping as I looked into my lap.

'So, what's the story then?' he asked, shifting back in his chair.

'Oh, I could give you a long story,' I said. 'To begin with, there's some post-traumatic stress involved, long-term homelessness, fear, ignorance, stupidity . . .'

I gave him a blow-by-blow of my fragmented working life, from picking tobacco, mopping floors, cleaning up fish guts, working on a prawn boat, mucking out horse stables, mowing lawns, working in a warehouse, gardening, labouring, being a nursing home janitor and cleaning shopping centres in the dead of night.

'It was heaps of little jobs all over the place, some in Queensland, some in New South Wales,' I explained. 'All for cash, which I'd spend, go broke and then I'd try to find another job. I'm feeling pretty bad about it now, to be honest with you, and I'd like to make arrangements to start paying back what I owe.'

Far from phoning the Australian Federal Police to take me away, the taxman smiled. 'Mr Smith, you're not exactly Christopher Skase,' he replied.

'Who?' I asked.

'Never mind.'

He told me that I was free to go and that we would start again from that day. I walked out of that office building as if floating on air. If a merciless government juggernaut like the Australian Taxation Office could forgive me and let me start afresh, anything was possible.

Exhilarated and fired up, I turned my attention to debts I owed to New South Wales and Queensland, mostly in the form of unpaid traffic fines, misdemeanours and infringement notices for drug offences – thousands of dollars all told. The States didn't show the same largesse as the ATO. Unable to settle the debts in one go, I negotiated to pay monthly instalments. It took me years, but I cleared the ledger and in return I was granted a feeling of complete freedom. By taking action I had removed another worry and, in doing so, I took another big step towards peace of mind. You cannot be contented with a bad debt hanging over your head.

All of the grace I'd received from people I had wronged made me realise how hypocritical I had been in not being forgiving as well. I had been a world champion grudge holder for much of my life – just ask Glenda. It had never occurred to me that harbouring bad blood was working against my own interests. Refusal to forgive is related to anger is related to resentment is related to hate – all of which had caused me immense pain for a very long time. Upon investigation, the only antidote I could find was not necessarily to forget what had been said or done to me, but absolutely to forgive.

Forgiveness is about *understanding* what happened. The people I most needed to forgive – Mum and Dad – had died long before I had this awakening. That didn't stop me going through the process of trying my best to understand what had occurred between us. I'd begun to think about them with a more open heart during my final days of living in the rainforest, and I continued to work hard on it after I got up off the park bench.

I concluded that I didn't have to agree with my parents' actions: I might acknowledge that they should have done better, but I came to understand they'd both grown up in trauma and had their reasons for doing what they did. Forgiving them was a huge and fundamental unburdening of pain – after all, they were the people who'd gifted me life and my name.

I should stress that this approach has worked for me but may not necessarily be helpful for everyone. I believe it's entirely possible to heal from trauma without needing to forgive, because I think for some people some things are unforgivable. If someone can come to terms with their own anger at a person, institution or injustices, then forgiveness is not necessary – so long as their pain ceases. Again, it's a complex area and I don't profess to have complete answers, just my lived expertise. When I think about the abuse I was subjected to in State care institutions, I don't believe I have any more pain around that. Those past experiences no longer impact me, and yet I don't know if I have forgiven them. I'm probably getting closer, but I will never forget.

There was just one person, however, who I thought I could never forgive. He was a particularly nasty piece of work: arrogant, thoughtless, rude, abusive, untrustworthy, vindictive, judgemental, self-absorbed, self-righteous, violent and extremely dangerous.

Yeah. Me.

A funny thing happened as I travelled around the countryside apologising for the awful things that guy had said and done. In talking to those I'd wronged and working things through with them, I gained a deeper understanding of myself, of where I was at the time and why I behaved the way I did. Acknowledging my faults was a pretty uncomfortable process and I took heart from an old piece of wisdom: 'To thine own self be true.' In other words, honesty starts from within. I had to be honest with myself in order to be honest and accountable with others.

If we're lucky, we are taught the fundamentals of honesty in our formative years. As children we're asked if we're telling the truth and encouraged to be honourable. If we're handed too much change, we're taught to resist deceitfulness and give the money back. I understood those forms of honesty right from the get-go. Self-honesty, however, took me half a lifetime to come to grips with. It is about much more than not telling lies or being equitable when handing out slices of cake. To become a better person, I had to find a new depth of honesty – a very critical, almost brutal self-appraisal.

My first experience of that level of honesty was admitting to myself that drugs and alcohol were causing me damage. For many years I lived in denial of that. I'd blame other factors and other people for my problem:

'I'm drinking because so and so made me angry.'
'I'm drinking because it's my last few dollars and I might as well enjoy it.'
'I'm using drugs because it calms my anxiety.'
'I'm getting stoned because it helps me think creatively.'

All abject lies told by me, to me.

By seeking to apologise to the world, I gained a better understanding, too, of the journey I'd been on since those bad old days. Only by mapping the roads travelled can I now say I'm a changed person. By acknowledging that I have done all I can to redeem myself, I've seen true forgiveness in action: forgiveness of oneself – an important foundation of contentment.

After taking a few hairy detours and negotiating some treacherous backroads, the old station wagon is out on the highway again. I know I'm going in the right direction these days because I'm in fairly heavy traffic, sharing the lanes with everybody else who's just trying to enjoy the ride. Most importantly, I no longer feel anxiety about the past. I know my lifetime of receipts are still there in the back seat because I have carefully placed them there in neat bundles, knowing I've taken care of what was owed. When I look in the rear-vision mirror today, it's a beautiful view.

CHAPTER SIX
WHY I'M HAPPY TO GET ANNOYED

I reckon anger is the cigarette smoking of emotions. It's toxic, self-destructive, offensive, socially unacceptable, harmful to others, it costs a lot and always leaves a bad taste in the mouth. It's also a mongrel to try to quit.

Next to fear, anger was the dark, destructive energy that pulsed through my circuitry for most of my life, and I gave in to it in just about any situation I felt didn't go my way. It wasn't only born of trauma, but I'd just never learned any other way to respond to injustice or offence, whether real or imagined. Anger and I go back a long, long way.

My father may have been the captain of our family ship, but he was no protector. Aside from the loose cannon I grew up to be, Dad was the most volatile and explosive person I have ever known. Mum wasn't too much better, and when the ill winds of their anger started to blow, violence almost always followed. If charity begins at home, so does all the bad stuff. It's no exaggeration to say that when it came to losing my temper, I was taught by experts.

By the time I was into my teenage years, I was absolutely at the mercy of my worst emotion – a problem that only grew worse down the track when I started drinking. Even as a boy, my angry outbursts could transmute into rage, resulting in physical or emotional carnage, and often both. I would say and do the most heinous things to people, whether they were a random, an acquaintance or someone I loved.

Not long before my fifteenth birthday I wound up back aboard the family frigate in Tamworth. I'd just been released from a stint in juvenile detention (on stealing charges), and after several harrowing months of incarceration I'd become fairly skittish. Although I'd hated every minute of being locked away with other frightened and troubled boys, I equally detested living back at home with Mum and Dad.

I started earning a little money doing odd jobs and, to provide myself with a distraction from the day-to-day chaos of the household, I saved up for an aquarium and stocked it with tropical fish. Even at that tender age, human beings were by far my least favourite life form; I much preferred the uncomplicated company I found in the animal kingdom. Watching my delicate fish friends slip silently through the water became my ritual escape. I'd zone out for hours in front of the aquarium. Sometimes I'd drift into a near trance-like state where no one could reach me.

One afternoon I was sitting in my room with the curtains drawn, transfixed by the fish, when one of my sisters innocently walked in, turned on the light and trilled, 'Hello!' She may as well have flipped the switch on a bomb. In a split second I leapt to my feet and became our father. The poor girl cowered in terror as I screamed abuse at her and savagely drove the heel of my shoe into the fish tank, knocking it over and smashing it to pieces. I have no recollection of the duration of the outburst, nor any memories of my asphyxiating fish gasping on the waterlogged carpet, only the moments before and the deep regret forever after. I guess that's why they called it blind rage – a state of mind I was destined to revisit often.

Not long after that episode I developed a new interest to occupy my troubled mind. Two interests, in fact: a second-hand motorbike and a local girl I was eager to impress. I rode it over to her house one day and tooled around on the street, hoping she'd see even just a little bit of James Dean in me. After showing off for a few minutes I managed to stall the thing. Multiple attempts to restart it failed, so I climbed off the bike, flung it to the ground and kicked the crap out of it, swearing at the top of my lungs all the while.

When I paused to take a breath, I heard the shocked voice of my hitherto potential girlfriend: 'Oh my god! If you get that angry with a bike, then I want nothing to do with you!'

Never heard from her again.

Whether my rage was directed at an inanimate object, my kid sister or a bikie in a pub, I always felt strong remorse once the smoke had cleared. What's more, every time I got angry, I lost. I seemed powerless, however, to stop it from happening again. The exhausting decades-long cycle of anger-eruption-regret on repeat wore a deep groove in the madly spinning disc of my psyche, and I struggled to control the emotion long after I left the park bench to start life anew.

Although I found practising forgiveness extremely effective when making peace with the past, it wasn't so useful in dealing with day-to-day frustrations. As with the evil nicotine, anger held an illusion of being self-soothing – especially where I perceived an injustice. 'I'm in the right, you have done wrong, and here's some indignant fury to drive the point home.'

Self-righteousness *can* feel empowering, for a little while anyway – right up until the moment you recognise that you've made a complete cretin of yourself in the process. Reflecting on past detonations also made me realise it was the people and things I cared about most that bore the worst of my wrath, like little sisters, colourful fish and the hope of having someone to love me.

Historically, anger was especially prevalent in my intimate relationships. A perceived hurt from someone I cared about could be far more painful than the worst abuse from a stranger. This stemmed from the fact that allowing people to explore the intimate spaces of my soul promoted vulnerability. Unguarded emotions live in that inner realm; an unobserved annoyance could easily sneak through undetected and before too long I'd say something I regretted.

Just as I knew every cigarette was slowly killing me, so it was with anger. It wasn't just the damage done in the initial outbursts either: anger leads to resentment – an ongoing state of grievance that's corrosive to the soul. I talk to people today who've had a similarly violent and abusive upbringing to me, and their lives have been ruined by the anger and resentment they have carried from their youth.

I know of others who died young because, one way or another those feelings overwhelmed them.

Left unaddressed, I worried that my uncontrolled anger would get me in the end, too. It would certainly impede my progress toward a contented life. I understood that I could never build a good character if I responded to challenging human interactions by blowing my lid. Try making and keeping friends if you're snappy, let alone seething at them through gritted teeth. As for holding on to grievances, I once heard it said that resentment is like drinking poison and waiting for the other person to die. At the time I'd never been told anything truer.

Although violence had exited my life the moment I stopped drinking, I remained a very, very angry person. Mostly it boiled away inside me, but it wasn't uncommon for me to lash out verbally when I detected an injustice, insult, stupidity or a threat. After every explosion, however, my old mate remorse would arrive on the scene within a matter of minutes.

'I don't want to be like this anymore.'

Unlike loneliness and acceptance, anger didn't fall into the category of an attitude I could actively change; rather, it is a powerful and universal human emotion. If I ever hoped to control mine better, a completely different approach was required.

Having never gone near a counsellor or psychologist at that time, I didn't know anger management courses even existed – not that I'd have sought any kind of professional help at that stage of my life. As with quitting drugs and alcohol, I would have to go it alone.

My DIY anger management strategy was to approach the problem the way a detective or researcher might. Whenever I lost my temper or felt anger welling up inside me, I'd conduct a post-mortem: a forensic search for the root cause and, hopefully, a solution. I'd begin with the basics:

'What caused it? What did the person say or do? Why did I react with anger? What did I say? How do I feel now? Was it worth it? How do I avoid doing it again?'

I quickly learned that just knowing the cause wasn't enough. Much more understanding was required, and I had to accept that my problem with anger wasn't going to be an easy fix. As with every other readjustment I'd faced since the epiphany, it was going to take some time.

I put countless angry episodes under the microscope and tried hard to push back against the next impulse to do my block but . . . *I still kept getting angry!* Cue frustration, another close and colluding cousin of Anger Gregory. I didn't seem to be getting anywhere. I could have easily given up after the first ten or twenty attempts to rein in the bucking bronco of an emotion. The years started flying by and I was still prone to outbursts.

Towards the end of my undergraduate studies in 2006, a person I knew quite well had developed a penchant for harassing me about my late-in-life education. He repeatedly cast doubt on my prospects of obtaining meaningful employment once I graduated. I couldn't control what this person thought or said, so I tried not to buy into it or react in any way. Since it was ongoing though, I had to ask him to drop it several times.

He kept it up, so I tried to manage the situation by avoiding him at every opportunity. Whenever we crossed paths, it seemed like he was deriving pleasure from taunting me. That's what pushed me over the edge.

The next time he started in on me, I went from annoyed to rage in a millisecond. Months of pent-up anger were released in a geyser of vicious words and half a litre of spittle. He was shocked and most definitely cowed.

When it was over . . . more regret.

When I subjected that outburst to forensic analysis later on, I realised that it wasn't like other episodes of so-called blind rage that left me clueless about the root cause. This eruption happened over time – in slow motion as it were – which allowed me to better understand what had taken place. I had allowed this person to influence my emotions with his jibes. I had effectively bought into what he was saying, because I was afraid he might be speaking a truth. His words had found a fear I carried deep inside me: that of failure and being unmasked as an imposter. I recognised, also, that the constant nature of the harassment reminded me of the way I used to be interrogated as a child. This was emotional gelignite: highly unstable stuff.

That self-understanding cleared a path that helped me make meaningful adjustments to the way I allowed conversations to impact me. While the spittle spraying episode was helpful, it was something of an anomaly: other eruptions happened quickly and for different reasons, and I struggled to understand what the triggers were – something I'd berate myself for on top of the regret I already felt.

I eventually realised my laboratory approach was missing something important – self-compassion. Rather than self-flagellate for a lack of progress, I decided I first needed to go easy on myself. I came to understand that there's no such thing as a failure when working in the anger management space. I decided I would treat every instance when I became angry with people or the world as a precious gift. I was being handed something new to dissect, analyse and process in my desire to not have it happen again.

Only when I was confident that I was in a self-forgiving frame of mind would I circle back to the basic question: 'What was the lead-in event or conversation that caused me to get angry?' I was surprised at how often I still drew a blank. A good example was the infamous call to Glenda, when all I could remember was her dig at my lack of common sense. It dawned on me, too, that I'd reacted that day by taking a huge swig of poison from the goblet of resentment. *'Right, Glenda! You've just won first prize in not being spoken to for the next fourteen years!'*

On most occasions when I got angry, I could only recall the broad brushstrokes of what was said in the heat of the moment. In retrospect I believe this 'anger amnesia' was my mind diluting and filtering the triggering external input in a way that let me cope with it at the time. It seemed to be a permanent feature of my anger response that I had no choice but to accept.

By re-joining society, however, other aspects of my anger came into sharp focus, such as the kinds of people who tended to provoke a response in me. I soon realised that there are a lot of different personalities out there, and

I wasn't going to get along with all of them. The main cul-
prits were racists, extreme-right wingers, narcissists, bullies,
homophobes and megalomaniacs.

I associate most of those types with injustice, which,
coming from my background, presses my anger buttons
in a very deep place. My anger management strategy with
regards to such people became one of avoidance: if I'm not
mixing with them, there's no problem. Since people don't
tend to wear T-shirts that tell you who they hate, one never
knows if someone's a racist or a homophobe until they start
speaking. In the past I would react to them with anger, but
over time I have learned that, if I'm unable to avoid them,
it's okay for me to release the valve by displaying a little
contempt instead. That, I realised, is the difference between
a reaction and a response.

If my post-mortems did nothing else, they gave me a clear
understanding of my different levels of anger. Level one of
anger is what I'd describe as irritation or annoyance. Garden
variety examples would include hearing people gossip
or rant about the same thing over and over, or when I'm
continually asked questions that seem to be without purpose. (I've recognised that this also triggers emotions of my
childhood from when I'd be interrogated by my parents,
teachers, police, nuns and wardens.)

When annoyance surfaces, I know my tolerance is being lowered – a reliable indicator that there's potentially trouble ahead. If I ignore or unwittingly bypass the early warning signs, as I'd spent half my life doing, I find myself pretty quickly at level two. There's any number of labels to describe that: furious, argumentative, aggressive, indignant, belligerent, bellicose. People experience and express signs of anger in different ways. To me it has the sensation of a chemical reaction – I can feel it flush through my body on a wave of adrenaline.

The next level is blind rage, an appalling state that exists on a more primitive plane of human behaviour. Blind rage is when you destroy an aquarium, stomp on a motorbike or headbutt someone in the skull. It is with a feeling of great contentment – and a bit of relief – that I can report I haven't felt that way in many years now, and I don't expect to again.

I still get angry, of course. We all do. It's one of the six universal human emotions written into our DNA alongside fear, surprise, disgust, sadness and happiness. But two of the things that have changed most in my life over the past twenty-three years are the weight I give to happiness and the control I have over anger.

Injustice remains a major trigger for me, and there are things I still don't like to talk about. I find in-depth discussion about my family of origin difficult, and I can't stand seeing people being spoken down to, degraded or humiliated. Rather than 'react' to the impulse, however, I 'respond' to it – in a far more measured way.

Nowadays I feel truly grateful when I start to feel annoyed because it immediately puts me in a position of control. Whenever I detect the subtle changes in my mood before the adrenal gland flares, I immediately lower the temperature by diving out the nearest window.

Ten to twelve years after leaving the forest, the people I'd chosen to have in my life noticed my metamorphosis from cranky old bastard into a more mild-mannered old bastard.

'You don't seem to get angry anymore, Gregory,' a colleague at university remarked once.

'Correct!' I responded. 'I escape out the window instead.'

She looked at me, puzzled.

'What I mean is that I allow myself to be cranky, grumpy, grouchy or annoyed – anything like that, so long as I don't go to the next level and get angry,' I explained. 'If I feel anger starting to come on, I'll walk out of the room, turn the sound down on the Zoom conference, excuse myself from the meeting, or whatever it takes to disengage until that feeling passes. So, yeah, I escape out the window.'

It's not always possible though, especially while serving on high level boards and in university governance roles, and even less so when working as an advisor to governments where, it gives me no pleasure to confirm, you come across quite a few idiots.

While I am well aware of my own shortcomings and know I have angered many people over the years, it is my experience that some people in bureaucracy achieve their positions not in spite of their limited capacity to think and work outside the square, but because of it. If you don't address their specific, restricted criteria and tick their bureaucratic boxes, you can easily find yourself in an infuriating stand-off. My field of expertise – trauma and homelessness – is a complex mosaic that doesn't lend itself to circumscribed thinking or bounded approaches. As a result I'm almost guaranteed to get annoyed with the box tickers, and sometimes anger is inevitable.

It has taken a lot of practice and discipline, but today when I move past annoyance and get angry, I can speak about it in a rational way. I can disagree – *respectfully* disagree – with people and speak my mind. I had to learn how to do that in order to keep my seat at the table at those higher levels of engagement. Oscar Wilde was a great help in that regard. He famously said, 'Sarcasm is the lowest form of wit . . .' Surprisingly few people bother quoting the second part: '. . . but the highest form of intelligence.'

I find sarcasm very helpful when dealing with some of the problematic people in government. Flippancy and sarcasm meshed together works well. I can point out to a person that they're being an idiot without malice or damage, and have them smile back at me and say, 'Thank you.'

Whether they register what my remarks actually mean after the meeting or whether they never give it a second thought, I have been able to express anger in a very controlled way and I get satisfaction out of that. It's another way of releasing the pressure valve without anyone else seeing the steam. After all, I have to work with these people. So rather than a headbutt, I just fire a shot right over their heads.

I'll say it again: there are a lot of different personalities out there. I'm not going to get along with all of them. Nor, I hasten to add, am I perfect. Far, far from it.

A few years back I was sitting in a dentist's waiting room in Coffs Harbour when I became enchanted by his exquisite, hand-woven Persian rug. Two thoughts crossed my mind: 'This guy makes a bit of money' and 'The person who wove this thing screwed up.'

For the most part the rug's swirling patterns were beautiful and orderly – as if imagined by a robot on hallucinogens – except for a section right in the middle that was slightly off-centre. Maybe not to the extent that everyone would notice, but I certainly did.

When my appointment came around, I hoisted myself into the dentist's fancy mechanical chair and remarked on his choice of waiting room décor. 'Your rug out there,' I began. 'It's a very beautiful rug.'

'Thank you,' he replied.

'Yeah, it's lovely but it's off-centre,' I added.

He smiled. 'That mistake is woven into it on purpose,' he said, wiggling his finger to put air quotes around the word 'mistake'.

'Oh yeah?' I replied, intrigued.

'Yes,' he continued, 'because the belief says "Only Allah is perfect."'

My rejection of religion aside, I loved the sentiment. As beautiful as that carpet was, its imperfection made it special. If it was a flawless facsimile of another rug, it would be just another surface to walk across.

In jettisoning, or at least trying to straighten out, my own flaws in my march towards contentment, I realised that I have a tendency to be obsessive-compulsive. It might sound paradoxical, but had you passed by me when I lived in the gutters of Sydney or in the forest, it would never have crossed your mind that inside my hunched shape lived a perfectionist. Yet I was one, and I still tend to be – though slightly less so since I first took a shine to my dentist's magic carpet.

In an academic context my 'good enough' was at quite a high standard. My Honours degree was first class, my Doctorate proposal was considered to be of such quality that it was widely shared with other PhD candidates as a good example. These were the fruits of an obsession with perfection. Over the years I have mellowed, though, and the only place I seek perfection in my life is in staying sober.

A sticker on my office door that says, 'Dare not to be perfect' is a daily reminder to me, as much as to anyone who comes to visit. I no longer obsess about things these days, and I have come to treasure my imperfections and those I see in others. They're what give us our singularity, our beauty and character – the good and the not so good.

I know for a fact that I will get angry again, most likely very soon. The age-old emotion will rise on a tsunami of adrenaline and I will look for a window to dive out of. When it happens, though, I can take comfort in the knowledge that it will recede again without me hurting anyone or raising the glass of poison to my lips.

CHAPTER SEVEN
PEELING LABELS

St Vincent's Hospital has been treating Sydney's sick and injured since 1857. Today the 400-bed institution straddles an entire city block that separates the red-light devilry of Kings Cross from the upscale terrace houses and wine bars of Paddington. To the residents of the affluent eastern suburbs and tens of thousands of CBD workers, St Vincent's is a sentinel. For a while it served as my local hospital too: I spent my days in the streets and alleyways that surround it and slept in public parks not far from where its shadows fell. A world-class facility it may have been, but I was never a big fan of the place, mainly because the people who worked there wouldn't let me die.

I last wound up in emergency at St Vincent's sometime during 1988–89. Kings Cross police had been called to a dirty stretch of pavement where, a concerned member of the public had reported, a man was prostrate and possibly dead. When the responding officers realised I was breathing, they roused me, which caused me to lash out and scream incoherently. Worried I was having a psychotic episode, completely out of my mind or overdosing on who knows what, the cops called for an ambulance and I was whisked to St Vincent's.

I don't recall exactly what I'd consumed that day, but if I had to take a guess it would have been a riotous amount of alcohol, a copious dose of amphetamines and probably a fistful of barbiturates, too. My mental state wasn't great at that time either – suffice to say I wasn't hospitalised simply for being drunk.

The ER staff had even less of a clue about what chemicals I might have imbibed and – since I kept demanding to be left alone to die – they didn't take any chances. Although I feebly tried to fight them off, they managed to feed me activated charcoal to absorb whatever mystery toxins I'd ingested. To make doubly sure I'd live to play another day, they pushed a rubber tube down my throat and into my gut to pump my stomach dry. It was a brief but horrendous stay in hospital. I was discharged the following morning, free to resume my life on the street.

Although annoyed about the medical intervention into my miserable existence, I felt a pang of embarrassment about my bombed-out behaviour, too. As a regular customer in emergency wards around the state, I knew only too well the stresses and demands hard-working medicos had to face every day. I cringed as I pondered what the dedicated staff at St Vincent's must have thought of me:

Alcoholic?
Mentally ill?
Addict?

The police who'd found me in the gutter had probably come up with a couple of choice descriptors for me too:

Dero.
Grot.
Pest.

Ah, labels. What were a few more? I'd been plastered with plenty by that stage in my life – every last one of

them negative. To the school kids in Tamworth I was Pus
Head (I had acne). In the classrooms I was judged to be
'stupid' (I was traumatised), and when I was sent to live in
the orphanage I was tagged as a 'problem child' (even more
traumatised by then). And at seventeen I was given an official, government-mandated label that stuck to me like mud
for thirty years to come.

After breaking into Mr Mitchell's house in 1973, I was
locked up in Sydney's Minda Remand Centre where, in
hindsight, I clearly displayed symptoms of post-traumatic
stress disorder – the painful wages of my childhood. Back
then, PTSD wasn't a diagnosable condition. In their struggle
to categorise certain behaviours, psychiatrists and psycholo-
gists did the best they could. One symptom of my trauma
had been an apparent outward absence of emotion. Unable
to pinpoint why I presented as blank, however, a New South
Wales government psychiatrist reached for a clumsy explanation. I was, he wrote in my official records, a 'personality
disordered adolescent, sociopathic type'.

I knew even less about PTSD than he did, so I not only
accepted the psychiatrist's misdiagnosis, I fully embraced it.
Being a sociopath explained why I always felt like a square
peg that had been hammered into a round hole: an outsider who couldn't make connections and was perennially

misunderstood. In a way, being labelled as defective gave me a raison d'etre.

'Hey! Check it out! I'm a sociopath!'

For someone who ultimately decided he wanted nothing to do with society, 'sociopathy' had its upsides. People were wary of me and kept their distance. Others were downright terrified, especially when I was on a rampage. No one wants to tangle with a 'violent sociopath'. As bogus as it turned out to be, I was a classic example of a person living their label.

We all do it at some stage in life. While some are placed on us by others, we also help create labels of our own. Some arise from the feedback we get in response to subtle messages we emit during our formative years. In a stable and loving environment, for example, you can expect to get stable and loving feedback designed to elevate your self-worth. You might think of yourself as a 'good kid', a 'hard worker' or a 'bright spark'. In a dysfunctional family you're more likely to get negative feedback, and your inner labels tend not to flatter.

Although I regarded myself as a bright and inquisitive little boy, I was called stupid a lot. Terrorised at home, I could barely function at school, where a succession of seemingly disinterested teachers wrote me off as a dunce. It was like tipping water on a fire. I heard 'stupid' so many times that my self-belief was eventually extinguished and I traded my inner-assessment for those of my parents and educators.

I lived the label of stupid for a long time despite never truly understanding what being stupid even meant. I still don't know what it's supposed to signify or how it is measured. Simply *believing* it, however, had a decisive influence over the shape of my life. 'Stupid' was a constant reminder that I was destined to fail, and since my supposed lack of intelligence had inoculated me against an upward trajectory through life, I figured my best efforts would always come to naught. If that was the case, then applying myself was a waste of time, so I downed tools. Why try if I was only going to lose?

I came to believe that I didn't deserve any kind of success. This spawned a lifelong tendency towards self-sabotage. As much as the inquisitive and ambitious side of my psyche would try to set some goals, the saboteur would stride in – often when I got close to attaining one – and shut the whole operation down. As soon as I could see the finish line in whatever I was striving for, I would quit. I was never there at the end to claim a reward.

When I was forced to leave high school at fourteen, I had the literacy and numeracy skills of a ten-year-old.

It's not that I was impervious to education, rather that I'd been handicapped by anxiety, depression, trauma and the deviousness of a master saboteur.

Alongside 'stupid', I soon picked up another label that took a lifetime to shake: 'shitkicker'. With scant education, no training and no trade under my belt I toiled in grimy jobs no one else wanted. Other men seemed to like having someone to look down on and were at pains to keep it that way. Any time I opened my mouth or tried to reach beyond my station, I was subjected to put-downs designed to keep me in my place. The one I hated the most was 'You're not paid to think.' That used to cut me very deeply. It was like telling me I had no right to an opinion. No right to my own thoughts.

In 1979, against all odds, I managed to climb the ladder just a little and rose to a slightly less degrading role at a Tamworth flour mill. I was earning reasonable money and, to my astonishment, I found myself with a girlfriend. As was the story of my life, however, Julie was in the driver's seat and I was just happy to go along for the ride. We'd met in Tamworth and after a whirlwind romance lasting a few months, we married and moved to Sydney to try our luck in the big smoke. Julie got a job in a department store, while I found work pushing a broom at a factory where better paid, more skilled men manufactured springs for car suspensions.

I slowly got to know one of the supervisors, a very nice fellow named Nathan. He'd chat with me during my breaks and, now and then, we'd even go to the pub after work where we'd exchange notes on life.

'You're actually quite a smart guy, Gregory,' Nathan remarked one afternoon. 'Why is it you're pushing a broom?'

'Because that's where I belong,' I replied. 'I'm a broom pusher. That's who I am.'

Living that label.

As the car spring business began to automate, a new computerised lathe was added to the workshop. It was a big deal: a couple of technicians had to fly out from Japan to install the high-tech gizmo. After they finished, I was standing around admiring it when Nathan sidled up to me. 'I reckon you'd be able to operate that,' he said, nodding at the lathe.

'Nah,' I demurred, shaking my head. He had to be kidding.

'No, I really do think you could handle it,' Nathan persisted. 'I'll show you how to run it and you'll get the hang of it. Trust me, you'll be fine.'

I was terrified. My role in life was to sweep up and clean toilets. It was the order of things, set in stone, and all of a sudden Nathan wanted to drag me out of it and pay me to think?

'I don't think so!'

The more I resisted, the more he insisted. I actually liked Nathan, though, so I eventually convinced myself to try to live up to his belief in me. It turned out he was right: over a few days I mastered the machine and suddenly rocketed up the charts from janitor to computer lathe specialist. I really liked the feel of that new label.

I was twenty-four years old and, for the first time in my life, I began to question whether I was indeed an idiot, and if my place in the world really was preordained. Looking back, Nathan's factory floor benevolence had demonstrated the value of positive input. For whatever reason he had taken an interest in me and, in doing so, elevated me. But although I went along with it for a while, I couldn't really buy into it or seize the opportunity because the rest of my life was falling apart at the seams.

By then I was a chronic alcoholic. As a result, my marriage was on the rocks before we'd even set sail. I'd get blind drunk every day and each night my young wife stepped through the door after work to either find me passed out or find herself on the receiving end of a barrage of wild accusations and verbal abuse. The crafty saboteur was hard at work, even when I was paralytic.

One day I came home to find that the locks to our apartment had been changed and our marriage was effectively over – just a short while after we'd tied the knot. I reacted by drinking myself into a woeful state of destruction. After winding up in Canterbury Hospital with a phantom head injury (I never knew what caused it), I was admitted to a psychiatric facility. When I was eventually discharged from there, I crawled away from Sydney with a few more self-imposed labels plastered on my back:

Divorcee.
Psych patient.
Loser.
Homeless man.

After I left the forest, it took me a long time to come to terms with all the labels that stood between me and contentment, let alone to begin the process of peeling any of them off. It would have been inconceivable had I not gotten off the drink and drugs first, particularly when it came to the biggest label: 'sociopath'.

An immediate benefit of gaining basic computer skills at community college was that I could finally research what was supposedly wrong with me. The Mayo Clinic describes sociopathy as a mental disorder '. . . in which a person consistently shows no regard for right and wrong and ignores the rights and feelings of others'. The more clarity of thought I gained through sobriety, the more I questioned the acumen of the erstwhile state psychiatrist. I *absolutely* understood right from wrong, and I had empathy, not just for human beings but for all living creatures. In the forest my greatest regret was that I'd killed animals for food. In the years after I left, I cried a river for them. Was that really the behaviour of a sociopath?

Others had a harder time dropping the labels they'd made for me. When I was around twenty-eight, I found myself once again in conflict with a bikie in Tamworth, only this time I'd picked a fight with a group of them. As I went to shoulder-charge the biggest fella, he pulled out a large shifting spanner and cracked me right between the eyes. It split my face open and knocked me out cold. I came to in hospital with a great vertical scar on my forehead that's still there today. Thankfully it has faded due to the softening power of age, but for many years whenever I got angry, it turned a vivid crimson.

Since I struggled with anger for years after leaving the forest, people tended to give me a wide berth. Often, though, I'd hear them talking about me in lowered voices in the soup kitchens.

'Psst. Look out, Charles Manson's just arrived.'
'Whatever you do, stay away from Charles Manson!'
'Charlie Manson never speaks . . .'

With the scarred forehead, the long beard and the mane of matted hair, apparently I was easy to pigeonhole as a psychopathic cult leader and mass murderer.

One of the interesting things about that label was that people noticed me. I wasn't invisible, so ultimately there was some advantage to being Charles Manson. As time progressed and I became more and more well, people finally knew who I was. They knew my trails, they knew that I would turn up on a Wednesday for lunch. They knew I was starting to look for work and improve myself. As I got better, I became more receptive to gossip. That's how I heard computers were the new thing, which led me to enrol in the IT course.

During my early years out of the forest, I became slightly more familiar with another homeless man who frequented the soup kitchens. I wouldn't say we were friends, but I was definitely good mates with his dog, and I always looked forward to seeing them. She was a lovely thing – a New Zealand huntaway cattle dog and a world champion tail-wagger. She made me feel instantly happy, as wagging tails tend to do, probably because I don't have one.

After not seeing them for a while, the bloke shuffled into the soup kitchen on his own one day.

'Where's your mate?' I inquired in a typical three-word grab, surprised not to see his faithful friend.

He looked at his feet, took a deep breath and replied in a low rasp. 'Hit by a car. Dead.'

I didn't know what to say. An awful feeling came over me: shock, confusion, sorrow and a strong compulsion to crawl into the nearest bottle. It was in that moment I realised that I had never learned to deal with grief. My immediate response to the loss of my fluffy pal was the same as it had always been: 'Go and get pissed and kill the pain.' Fortunately, I'd been practising for such moments.

'I don't drink and I don't use drugs.'

It was the first time in my life I faced anguish or heart-break without drinking myself into a blackout. With nowhere to run and hide emotionally, I had no choice but to think about the dog and what she had meant to me. My heart went out to her owner too for the agony he must have been going through. In the dunes I cried for them both.

Over several weeks I noticed my sadness over the man and his dog morphing into something else – acceptance.

I was closing in on fifty and I knew death was part of life; I'd been close enough to it myself many times, after all. I meditated on the fact that nothing lasts forever. 'Just as each day has a beginning,' I consoled myself, 'so it has an end.'

It was a key philosophical awakening about the finite nature of being. I knew one day I wouldn't be, and that only made my days more valuable. Understanding that helped me to slow down and appreciate the conversations and interactions I'd started to have with people. It helped me nurture relationships that then flourished – a development that ultimately allowed me to refute and reject the state psychiatrist's useless categorisation of me. After all, a sociopath doesn't care about his family, friends and even strangers and their little dogs.

Still, the sociopath tag took longer than you'd think to fade into nothingness. Indeed, the removal of all the unhelpful labels was a long and sometimes painful process. It required introspection, reckoning with the past, making significant emotional adjustments to the present, and managing countless external factors. Along the way I never overlooked the incredibly good fortune I had to experience my park bench epiphany. Had I not, I likely would have worn my negative labels all the way into an early grave and been buried with them.

Having been given a second chance in life, I recognised I had two options: I could manage the problems behind the labels, or I could deal with them head-on. If I chose management I'd have basically said to myself, 'I've got symptoms for the rest of my life and I'll just try to work through as best I can.' A lot of people do that, but I don't think that's where contentment lies. To reach that place, I needed to go deep inside and change the fundamental settings by individually addressing each underlying problem.

The first question I needed to ask myself was 'Why?' For example:

'Why am I angry?'
'Why am I an alcoholic?'
'Why am I lonely?'

In asking those questions I acknowledged that the issues existed, they were a problem and I was taking ownership of them. Answering honestly allowed me to probe and understand the problems. The reasons I struggled with anger, alcohol and loneliness stemmed from childhood trauma.

This answer led to more questions: 'If it was childhood trauma, what were the traumatic events? Who was behind them and why, and how do I want to feel about that going forward?'

Only by pulling each problem apart could I begin to understand myself and determine my own worth according to the facts, not my tattered coat of labels. The approach has worked for me, but I have to stress again that I have no qualifications in this space other than my own experience. Everyone is different.

Today my work in the vulnerability space is a constant reminder of how hard it can be to change. Take people living with the label 'rough sleeper'. When governments or agencies intervene to help a person out of rough sleeping, they need to do it within the first six weeks, because that's when people generally still have connections to their previous lifestyle. After six weeks, helping them becomes more difficult.

Once someone has been rough sleeping for twelve weeks, they're in survival mode: new life patterns and new skills have taken over – survival skills. Once a person enters that mindset, it's very difficult to get them out and far more complicated. They become participating members of a different community – that of rough sleepers. It has its own set of rules and its own grapevine. To access it, one needs to be able to speak the language and that's not something you can find in a textbook.

At that point helping them is no longer about resources or providing a place where they can be safe: it's about changing mindsets, overcoming loneliness and confronting despair. Once your days are purely about survival, there can be fear around the idea of stepping out of it. People become risk averse because at least in their current situation they know what they've got, they know where they can get a feed and, sometimes, they know where there's a place to sleep that's reasonably safe. Within sixteen weeks they're living a new label they probably never saw coming: homeless.

With those labels, however, come excuses, justifications and rationalisations. I have met thousands of people suffering poverty and homelessness and found the majority to be very intelligent and resourceful. No matter how clever they are, many get stuck in a certain way of thinking that aligns with the labels they've been given or have given themselves. As a social researcher I'm working hard on possible solutions to this problem. I know not everyone has a cathartic moment that causes them to change the way they think. I was lucky to have had mine, which is why I'm always prepared to publicly share my experiences and the lessons I've learned.

*

People still try to label me today. While I'm a relative new-comer to the town of Orange, my partner, Catherine, seems to know every second person on the street. She's been an educator and has owned three businesses in the city, writes for a well-read regional glossy magazine and sings in bands. This is on top of being a mum and having a day job as a senior business controller, accountant and human resources manager. Just about every time we go out, we run into someone she's either worked with or rocked with onstage.

It was Catherine who first pointed out that many people have the same initial reaction to me: total confusion. I see it now, too. They squint a little as they try to assess the long-haired, bearded man in front of them and search for a label. The very first thing they tend to say is, 'So, what do *you* do?'

That's a loaded question, and in years gone by it could easily have earned them a headbutt to the bridge of the nose. Now that I'm older, wiser, sober and fully aware of why they're asking, I quite enjoy these moments. Any time some-one asks me, 'What do you do?' I answer, 'As little as possible without getting caught.'

Catherine will usually follow up with an actual answer: 'Oh, don't mind him, he's an academic.'

The change of label in those moments is instant and definitive. The expression on their face does a one-eighty and all of a sudden they think they're looking at a different person. They're not, though – it's still me, but the label they thought they had for me is useless.

Losing my unwanted labels has been hugely liberating. After leaving the forest I decided I would always 'be there at the end'. I would finish whatever I started, and it was only through the process of completion that I was able to overcome my self-sabotage. A large part of developing the habit of succeeding was understanding why I self-sabotaged in the first place. I wrote it all down to try to unravel it, and in the end everything came down to the external labels I had received as a child:

'You are dumb.'
'You'll never amount to anything.'
'You don't measure up.'

I overcame self-sabotage by setting small goals and building an attitude of completion. I didn't suddenly launch into an Honours degree or PhD: I started with little things like completing the form to apply for my driver's licence or get a PO box. I found it difficult, and in days past I would have tossed the pen and given up halfway through. But one completed task led to another, and another after that.

The journey could sometimes be scary. It took a long time to become comfortable with being there at the end. Nowadays when I complete something, though, I feel extremely satisfied. I feel like I've earned the label 'reliable'.

While we can't always avoid labels, we can choose which ones we hang on ourselves. Nowadays, the basics are important to me. I don't expect new people I meet to know I hate being called Greg. Whenever someone does, however, I make sure I tell them straight away, 'That's not my name. My name is Gregory.'

There are many others I'm happy to wear today: father, friend, academic, sociologist, lived experience expert, specialist consultant. I embrace these not only because they are of my choosing, but because they send a signal that I'd like to contribute to society. After all, I have a lot of lost time to make up for, and I know the crazed Gregory with a tube down his throat in St Vincent's could never have comprehended how much worth was left in his life.

In May 2022, I was invited to a two-day retreat to speak to senior medical staff from St Vincent's Hospital. The director of casualty and his team were eager to hear my thoughts on problems they were encountering with violent patients posing a danger to staff in the ER, particularly with respect to drug and alcohol abuse. As a lived experience expert, I knew exactly what they were talking about and exactly what they needed to hear – the hard, unvarnished truth.

'The simple fact is those patients don't care about you,' I explained. 'When your staff are being injured or frightened or abused, that's of absolutely no concern to them. You have to understand that these are really angry people. They're using drugs and alcohol to kill an internal suffering. If they want to die and you're trying to save them, they're going to be pissed off with you.'

It was a blunt but necessary opening gambit, and over the next two days I fielded dozens more questions from some of the country's top medicos as they searched for better outcomes in the often fraught and confounding crossroads of the ER. They sought my lived experience input again in 2023, this time at the National Inclusive Health Strategy planning day. It was my absolute pleasure and honour to attend. I feel like I owe it to them, too. After all, they had refused to let me die.

CHAPTER EIGHT
THE THREE-DAY WEEK

I had no proper knowledge of time when I lived in the rainforest. Rarely did I know what day of the week it was, or the month. There was a confounding period in the late 1990s when I didn't even know what year I was living in. In my peculiar world, 'the time' was simply a matter of early or late, day or night – nothing more. Seconds, minutes and hours were as useful to me as they were to the critters I shared the landscape with. Like the insects and snakes, I had no schedule. I was never ahead of time or running behind it: I arrived where I was going whenever I got there.

After ten years had crept behind me, that turned out to be nowhere.

As with everything of value, the human race has commodified time. There may be almost eight billion of us on the planet – each with our own quirks, skills, talents and foibles – but the universe unbiasedly grants all of us exactly the same ration of hours. Whether you're a tech billionaire or a broom pusher, you get twenty-four a day and not a second more. Time is one of humanity's few common denominators. It's how we use our allotment that sets us apart.

When I lived in the forest, I thought I had all the time in the world and I lived my life accordingly. I could do next to nothing for days and then suddenly embark on a whimsical resupply trip into the towns, usually setting off on an empty stomach and with a full water bottle in the stillness of dawn, when the bush was at its most magical. I could spend an entire morning dawdling just a few hundred metres along the trails before meeting the road. Expeditions into Mullumbimby or Byron Bay could last a day, a few days or a week or more. With no clock running, I would trudge back home to the forest whenever the universe said it was time to.

During long years around my campfire, I also mastered the art of time travel. I'd gaze into the dancing flames, crack open the bedroom door of my childhood and spend hours wandering around in 1965 in search of clues to why my parents had chosen to terrorise and then abandon me. I spent eons reliving the seventies and eighties, too – retracing the painful footsteps that had caused me to flee to the outermost margins of society.

We're all time travellers, of course, but really only in one direction. In the blink of our mind's eye we can sail back through the ether and lose ourselves in the doings of yesteryear. I suspect, however, that people from a background of trauma are more practised at this than most.

Despite the fact that it almost killed me, I was very fortunate to have quarantined myself from society for ten years. With hindsight I recognise that I needed that time alone to start to come to terms with some of the trauma I'd experienced. Indeed, one of the complexities in treating mental illness is that it takes time – lots of it – for people to recover and readjust to life. My recovery took decades, something many people experiencing PTSD need in order to separate themselves from the retraumatising of their past. Because we place so much value on time, especially monetary value, it's difficult to find that time. When money is involved, the clock is always ticking – even on recovery.

While I was able to separate myself from society, I know that's not a viable option for most people who suffer from

PTSD, including my fellow Forgotten Australians. Although I didn't do it knowingly, and even though I caused myself a lot of harm along the way, the decade when I wasn't retraumatising myself by being shamed and stigmatised was the beginning of my eventual recovery.

In the forest I was able to reflect on my past at my leisure – without expectation and without answering questions. I was able to understand and come to terms with a lot of the things that had happened to me and ultimately realise that I had to stop blaming others for them. It was only after I walked out of the forest to give society another chance that the clock restarted and I realised I'd already inadvertently laid some of the groundwork for a better life.

It was the noisy, diesel-driven conveyor belt of public transport that dragged me back into sync with Australian Eastern Standard Time. Although I did a lot of walking in the early years post-epiphany, my as yet undiagnosed hepatitis left me with low energy, so if I wanted to travel more than a kilometre or two, I had to take part in the great bus ballet. Although I hadn't owned a watch since forever, my newfangled Ericsson brick phone featured a digital clock. Armed with the mobile and bus timetables for the Northern Rivers and the Gold Coast, a measure of routine returned to my life.

Some of the routes that criss-crossed my haunts in the borderlands could see an hour or so lapse between buses. If I wanted to be at a certain place by a certain time – such as TAFE for the beginning of a lesson or the RPSCA for the patting of some cats – I absolutely had to connect with the right chauffeur-driven Mercedes. All I had to do in order to ruin my entire day and trigger an anxiety attack was fart about in my campsite in the morning and miss a bus. The same applied at the soup kitchens. Want to go hungry? Turn up late.

Being on time wasn't just a matter of paying attention to the blinking digits on the Ericsson, it required a complete overhaul of the modus operandi – or rather lack thereof – that I'd followed over the previous twenty-five years. To be on time was to be organised and prepared, which essentially meant caring about my future. After a while my newfound attention to time led to a profound realisation.

It occurred to me that time was a lever I could pull to control my emotions and protect my mental state. I had the power to unleash the destructive forces of shame, anger, depression and anxiety simply by not bothering to organise my time. By the same token, I discovered that I also had the executive clout to make myself feel comfortable, observative, productive and contented for the day – all I had to do was be punctual or, even better, early.

I grew embarrassed to think that for the longest time I had scoffed at the suits with tidy hair for being 'slaves to the clock'. All the while I had casually let the sands of time cascade through my fingers with nothing much to show for it except dirty shoes. Coming to understand that time is as precious as air was a game changer for me.

One of the vows I'd made after the epiphany was to never commit another criminal offence for as long as I lived. Nor would I harm or take advantage of another person in any way. I refused to engage in deception, and stealing was out of the question. Still, I was eager to bring in a bit more money to supplement the disability support I was receiving and keep me stable while I studied. Since I'd been knocked back from every single job I applied for after leaving the forest, I had to get creative.

As a drifter, I'd always been drawn to community markets: makeshift shopping centres for a makeshift man. One Sunday morning in 2002 I found myself mooching around a funky little market in the grounds of the Tweed Heads Police Citizens Youth Club. With nothing else to do the following weekend I figured I'd pay the $10 site fee at the PCYC, set up a stall and see what happened.

During my daily wanderings, I was often amazed at the quantity and quality of household items people jettisoned during council clean-ups. Ramshackle mounds of society's excess stuff would appear on the footpaths: couches, tables, lawnmowers in need of a spark plug, surfboards with just a ding or a missing fin, wine racks, ironing boards and bikes that needed a dollop of TLC. These were the items I salvaged and put up for sale at the market. For the first time in years, I began to exchange my time for money and other riches.

I took to selling wares like a duck to water. As with all commerce it required good time management, and I was punctual and organised, but I still struggled to converse with the parade of complete strangers. Sometimes to try and relax, I'd let my mind drift and imagine myself as a trader in a grand Byzantine bazaar. I encountered all kinds of interesting people on those Sundays, and after a while I began to look forward to the next market day. I also started to make some cash, which is how I could afford a fairly busted-up Mitsubishi van. I couldn't exactly store the stuff I'd liberated from council clean-ups in the dunes, so I needed somewhere to warehouse it during the week. The van was the answer to that problem, and it allowed me to broaden the scope of my operations to the more lucrative world of garage sales. As an added bonus, it provided me with a dry place to sleep when it really poured with rain.

I'd started scouring local noticeboards and newspaper ads for upcoming garage sales and made sure I arrived an hour before the scheduled time to get the pick of the crop before anyone else. Typically I'd park out the front of houses in Tweed Heads, Coolangatta or the Gold Coast, scurry inside and load up with any gear I could see dollar signs in before hightailing it to another property in search of more treasures. Watching the clock was crucial: I had to wake up extra early to get the proverbial worm. Later on I'd tidy the goods up, double the price and – when Sunday rolled around – I'd be open and trading at the bazaar.

After four very successful weeks, I had to rent a storage unit in order to warehouse the growing inventory of stock. I'd spend my Saturdays there giving the wares a spit and polish and loading the van so I'd be ship-shape and Johnny-on-the-spot the following day. My fastidiousness paid off. After two months, the powers that be at the PCYC offered me a permanent site in a prime location, which I politely accepted. More than anything, I was chuffed at the gesture of social inclusion.

Market day became the outright highlight of my week. I'd fly a big Chinese dragon flag over my stall so everybody knew where I was. I sold all manner of things, from the ubiquitous second-hand (or third- or fourth-hand) bikes, surfboards and wetsuits to books, glassware, knick-knacks and furniture. I even offloaded a couple of boats.

As well as boosting my meagre estate, the markets helped me become more socialised. In the beginning I was edgy and self-conscious, but as I gained confidence I not only did a better trade, but I had a bit more fun. The burgeoning sense of self-worth was only made possible by a reciprocal respect for my fellow human beings.

At one garage sale I paid $50 for a spent brass artillery casing that had supposedly come from the ill-fated cruiser HMAS *Sydney*. The waist-high shell took pride of place on my stall table the following week, but I didn't put a price tag on it. Sure enough, it got people's attention, especially the ex-military types.

'How much do you want for it?' I was asked on the first day.

'Nothing. It's not for sale,' I'd reply.

'I'll give you $150 for it right now.'

'Sorry, it's really not for sale.'

A week later a young bloke offered me $300.

'Nup,' I said. 'It's a display item. It's too valuable to sell. It's from HMAS *Sydney*! I couldn't possibly let it go.'

He returned the following Sunday and slammed $400 on the table. I ummed and ahhed, squinted through one eye and scratched my head. Finally I agreed that he could have it for $400 – but only if he promised to take special care of it. It was a good lesson in the notion that the more you tell people something's off limits, the more they've got to have it.

The best haggle I ever had, however, was with a young Swedish woman. She was on the hunt for a surfboard and the one I had for sale had caught her eye. I'd picked it up at a garage sale for $30 and stuck a $75 price tag on it, with the expectation of letting it go for around $60.

She checked the board over as if she was a qualified assessor in white gloves and we were at a Christie's auction. She wasn't fooling me though – we both knew the board was in good nick.

'What do you say to $30?' she asked.

'Sorry, were you talking to me?' I responded (part of my schtick).

'Yes. I'll give you $30 for this board.'

'It's worth more than $100 new,' I replied.

She huffed a little and left but didn't stray far. Her eyes kept drifting to the surfboard. She circled back intermittently during the morning, and we went to and fro a little more.

'Would you take $35?'

I shook my head. At lunchtime a fellow marketeer offered me $70, but by then I'd labelled the board 'not for sale'. I was playing games with my new Swedish friend.

Finally she confronted me. 'Look, I have to leave now. I will give you $40.'

I couldn't bring myself to torture her any more, so we shook on it and she skipped away with the board tucked under her wing, no doubt to keep an appointment with the ocean. Although I only made a measly ten bucks on the surfboard, my true profit for the day was a protracted interaction with a pleasant stranger. Progress.

I got to know a few of the other traders, too, and picked up the odd treasure from them, including an old-fashioned fob watch I kept in my pocket for the times when the Ericsson ran out of charge. It was a lovely looking timepiece, but it lost half an hour each day which, ironically, made me even more conscious of the time as I was constantly having to reset it.

When I first emerged from the forest the days – and buses – seemed to move at such a pace that I worried I was running low on time. In the two decades since, however, I have come to understand that, for me at least, there's no such thing as 'enough time,' 'not enough time' or 'too much time.' It's all just time and, like everyone else, it's what I do with it that matters.

Today I have strategies for maximising the impact of my time. Following a life of utter chaos, it came as a bit of a surprise to discover that I'm a pretty good planner – something I first learned about myself while running after buses. Nowadays I hate being late for anything. Being late reflects poorly on my self-management and shows disrespect for the situation and the people I'm meeting with.

Over the past few years there have been many more demands on my time outside of family responsibilities. I'm required to travel a lot professionally, often to places I've never been to before, to speak and consult at scheduled events. No matter where I go, I make sure I arrive early and do a reconnoitre of the venue well ahead of the starting time. I even do this if I'm in town a day early; only after that will I take some time to enjoy myself, see the sights or boot the computer up and get some work done. Pulling the reins on my time in that way makes me feel secure and confident that I won't let people down or make a poor impression straight off the bat.

Even when I go to a doctor – possibly the worst profession when it comes to running late – I'm always early.

Add that buffer to the guaranteed lateness of the doctor and I can wait up to an hour for my appointment to begin, but I never consider it a waste of time. There is always something productive to do when you're early. Technology allows us to work, read, communicate or plan how we're going to use the rest of our day. I can even use that time to switch off or have some quiet reflection should I choose to.

You really can never be too early – there's no such thing. I can arrive a week ahead of a meeting or an engagement and find I've still got plenty to do. If you're late, however, you're immediately playing catch-up and the consequences include anxiety, shame, embarrassment and depression. Like a wise man once said, 'If you want to feel bad . . .'

Being late is a bad thing in my book, and I've seen it bring plenty of people unstuck. As a university lecturer I have observed the time management of thousands of people up close. Students who turn up on time and manage the hours in their day will almost always achieve good results. Being an educator in a structured system, I know as well as anyone that life can sometimes get in the way of a well-planned day: tyres go flat, kids get sick and keys are lost. It happens and I accept that. Then there are students who are *habitually* late. The simple fact is that they don't perform anywhere near as well as those students who are not.

This has nothing to do with intellect. You can be the smartest person in the room, but if you can't properly manage your most valuable commodity, it's impossible to invest it in getting good results. Even when COVID-19 forced us out of lecture theatres and online, some students were chronically late to my lectures. Unsurprisingly, they tended to be the same students who had a pack of dogs at home eating their homework and five or six grandparents who'd recently passed away. When those students either failed completely or fell short of what they'd hoped to achieved, they'd opened the door to feeling bad.

One afternoon quite early on in my sobriety I found myself sitting on the beach at Coolangatta doing a bit of time travel. I was immersed in the misery of being locked under the stairs in St Patrick's Orphanage. I felt myself on the brink of a major depression.

> *'Why do I feel like this? Where is it coming from?'*
> *'Why am I haunted? These things happened more than thirty years ago!'*

It struck me that I was actively making myself depressed by choosing to dwell on past events I had no control over.

And yet there I was, sitting on a world-famous beach on a beautiful afternoon, stone-cold sober and with a promising education well underway.

'What happens if I just stop, start looking around at what's happening now and not think about the past?'

I was reminded of the sign I'd seen outside a church a month or so earlier. 'Now is the greatest gift of all. That's why they call it The Present.'

Just like getting sober, living in the moment required a lot of practice. Whenever demons called out to me from the past, I pulled myself into the present moment by being mindful of the world around me. I tried to slow every second down and focus only on what my eyes could see, what my ears could hear and what my body could feel.

Over time my default started to shift, even though I'd not had much of an idea how to start. Like everything else in my life, mindfulness was a DIY affair. For years I used to wonder, 'How do you meditate? What *is* meditation?' I'd half-heartedly tried different techniques, like listening to the waves and focusing on a waterfall. Over time I realised that, for me, meditating was just about being still and listening. If I'm quiet for a moment I can hear the birds, I can hear a dog barking, wind in the trees or kids in a park kicking a footy around. Those sounds centre me in the moment.

'They are real and they are happening now.'

An interesting thing about the mind is that we can only think about one thing at a time. So if I'm focusing and disciplining myself to hear the now, I'm simply not thinking about the past.

I still had to deal with periods of frustration and depression, but by trying my best to live in the present moment, I experienced far less depression about *the past* than I ever had before. The same applied to my levels of anxiety, which were usually fuelled by my unhelpful attempts at time travel to the future.

'What if I fail my exams?'
'What if I can never get a job?'
'What if people don't forgive me?'

When I stayed in the present moment, those concerns vanished into thin air.

'Everything is exactly as it is meant to be, right here, right now.'

I don't want to live in yesterday, and tomorrow will always be a day away, so I can't live there, even though I can plan for it. So I like to live in today, and more specifically in the now. That's the essence of mindfulness: a meditation on the clarity of the present moment. That takes practice and a fair bit of attention. Obviously the past and future play an important role in the human condition, but spending too much time there can ruin today.

For this reason I reject the notion of the seven-day week, and have instead adopted a three-day week comprising yesterday, today and tomorrow – the only three days I concern myself with.

If I'm living in the past, I'm just creating angst for myself. If I'm living in dreams of the future, they may never come true: more anxiety, more fear. If I live in today, I've got much more control over who I am, what I'm doing and where I'm going. That doesn't mean I forget about yesterday. That doesn't mean I don't dream about tomorrow, but functioning in today – and really focusing on it too – is far more exciting, productive and fulfilling.

I cite the three-day week as one of the reasons I excelled in tertiary education. By operating in that small parcel of mental and emotional time, my mind rarely wandered from the task at hand. Whenever I attended a lecture or a workshop, I took my 'now' with me. Nothing else existed — only what was happening right in front of me. I had fun doing that, too, and I quickly learned that if I was having fun and enjoying what I was doing, I had more chance of remembering what I'd learned. If I didn't enjoy it then, by default, I wouldn't want to be there. And if I didn't want to be there, chances were I wouldn't remember the content.

Everything starts with being present. I defy any person to live outside of the now. If you can live in the past and be successful, I'll be impressed. If you can live in the future and kick goals, I'll be blown away. It's only by living in the now that most of us can thrive.

This doesn't mean the length and breadth of our lives are unimportant or to be forgotten. One of the most important parts of today is understanding how I got to this moment where I am typing these words. I got here by living every day of my past. If I was to reject that, I'd be putting holes in my now. As much trauma as I experienced in the past, it is priceless because that pain informs the decisions I make and carry into tomorrow. Today is the flame, the catalyst between the past and the future, and it shines brighter than they ever will.

*

In addition to the push and pull from our memories and our hopes, we're under a lot of societal pressure to not be in the moment. Corporations want us to live in the future, a glittering place where their products and services will make us happy, for a price. Meanwhile governments – especially conservative ones – tend to want us to live in their versions of the past, whether real or contrived, to legitimise narratives and policies. My advice? Don't let anyone tell you what time it is – know it for yourself and go at the pace that works best for you.

A while back I posted a meme on social media that said, 'Never discourage someone who's making progress, no matter how slow.'

In response a Facebook friend asked, 'What about someone who makes no progress or even goes backwards? Is there any encouragement for them?'

The first thing that came to mind when I thought about a response was time itself. Time does not go backwards. Sometimes we may feel like we're not making progress and even going backwards, but by time's definition we're always making headway through space.

Having said that, progress can sometimes involve circling back emotionally and re-experiencing feelings to gauge where we have come from. Sometimes I've needed to relive unpleasant feelings many times over before I've been able to step through them and keep moving forward. Most recently, that related to feeling like a fraud: that I didn't deserve or have the right to be in the positions I now occupy. I felt insecure for a long time, but I now understand that casting that critical eye over my journey is how I progress.

When I was studying, there were countless times that I felt I wasn't getting anywhere. I had to learn not to be too judgemental of myself (and thus cause more problems) and to trust that I was doing the right thing and that my motives were good. If my motives were good, it didn't matter if I felt stuck. Feelings are not always facts. They can deceive. A feeling of going backwards is a feeling – it's not necessarily true.

I learned that slow progress is better than no progress. Sometimes when we're taking very small steps and we can't see that we're making progress, the people around us can. That's why it's good to have conversations with someone in your close orbit. It's important to have that objective perspective. Most importantly, we need to remember that unless we work out how to turn back time, we are all hurtling into the future together.

*

On my fiftieth birthday – two years into my undergraduate degree – I was called into Centrelink for a review of my disability support pension. The government had brought in a doctor and I was asked to justify why I should remain on a government pension.

'Well, I guess I don't have to,' I began. 'The truth is I could probably go out and get a job as a brickie's labourer tomorrow, but I'm fifty years old and I might last five years doing that.

'On the other hand I've got two years left on my degree. If I take the two years to finish that, I'll likely get a job more conducive to my physical ability and I'll last in the workforce for a lot longer.'

There were a few beats of silence before the doctor clapped his hands and said, 'Sold! Stay on disability.'

That episode wasn't about a desire to remain on welfare for the sake of it, it was purely about the best use of my time – from my perspective and that of the wider community too. Ever since I started reconstruction on myself in 1999, I'd always known I wouldn't be on a disability pension for the rest of my life. I've been under my own steam now for almost twelve years, having also paid off my HECS debt, and I'm glad my taxes contribute to others in need of the helping hand of welfare.

Now that my days are so full, I've found one of the challenges of living in the present day is that sometimes I don't remember what I'm supposed to do tonight! I've gone from having nothing to do for years to sometimes struggling to find a spare twenty minutes. That's why a diary has become such an important tool in my life.

One thing I never have to diarise is the time I spend with my family, my friends and – just as importantly – myself. Without fail I take a few moments out of each day to separate myself from the world. It might be a walk around the block, sitting quietly on my own or going out into the yard to check on the chooks. It's a time when I can review what I have control over and what I don't. Sometimes I'll kick off my shoes and socks and savour the feeling of the grass between my toes.

'This is real.'
'This is my moment.'
'This is my world.'

Then the time comes when I have to go back through the door and enter the matrix again.

Although there are only three days in a week, I've realised how important it is not to rush some things. In the early days of my recovery, I fixated on some of the old clichés about time:

'Go with the flow.'
'Enjoy the view.'

I decided to combine them and came up with a cliché all of my own: 'Put the paddle in the canoe, go with the flow and enjoy the view.'

If I was pushed to give my philosophy on life, that would probably be it. After all, I had paddled against the flow for most of my life and rarely got anywhere. Maybe it's just another way of saying 'be in the moment', but it feels like something more. When I look back over my education, this is exactly what I did. I put myself aside and allowed it to happen. Each of my achievements nominated me for the next one. I did not have to want, demand or manipulate. After each project, if I qualified, the next would present itself. This continues to happen in my life. The less I am involved, the more I enjoy the proceeds of simply being the best man I can be for the time I have left.

CHAPTER NINE
OH, BOY

One essential for my hermit life was a wide-brimmed hat. Over the years I cycled through plenty. Whenever my latest lid succumbed to sweat and the humidity of the rainforest, I'd walk into Mullumbimby or Byron Bay and pick up a replacement at an op-shop. I had some great ones over the years, but my absolute favourite was a black felt number. It wasn't only comfortable and gave good sun protection, it served an important psychological function, too. After a particularly stoned night of metaphysical contemplation, I resolved to stick different coloured sewing pins along the circumference of the brim. The tiny plastic satellites in orbit around my skull were meant to remind me that I wasn't the centre of the universe.

Aside from helping me manage trauma, the unlimited supply of time I found in the forest allowed me to have in-depth philosophical conversations with myself ranging from topics of morality, ethics and integrity to cosmology, religion and justice. One major realisation I had while mulling over those was the fact that for most of my life I had seen myself as occupying the centre of all creation.

Trauma and addiction had hard-wired my self-centredness and self-absorption, and I had to admit I generally looked at human interactions as transactional at best, and opportunistic at worst. I was always subconsciously asking the question, 'What can you do for me?' This was rapaciousness borne of survival – an interpersonal form of hunting and gathering whatever I needed to see me through each day.

Even back then I knew that was no way to live, but as a recluse and an addict, I didn't know what to do about it other than turn my headwear into a model of the galaxy. It wasn't until I was back in the company of humans full time – drug free and sober – that I truly started to come to grips with my self-centredness. All I'd needed was a little nudge.

In my experience, the down-and-outers of the world have a lot to teach us. I'd picked up plenty of treasures by eavesdropping on gravelly conversations in soup kitchens: profound insights about life and death, love and hate, good and bad, and everything in-between. The lessons weren't always simple or clear straight away, like the snippet I overheard that taught me the difference between being selfish and being self-centred.

I was hunkered low over my tea and toast one morning when I heard a hefty Kiwi guy share a frank self-assessment with another bloke. 'One of the things I've learned about myself is that if you meet me, you're gonna lose,' he said evenly. 'If you meet me it's gonna cost you. It might cost you a cigarette, it might cost you some money, it might only cost you your time . . . doesn't matter: whatever it is, you're paying up.'

Even though he oozed a bravado bordering on menace, it was a surprisingly raw and honest thing to say. If you took him at his word, the big New Zealander was the definition of self-centred. To him, human beings were mere tools whose only purpose was to serve his needs. His words rang in my ears for days afterwards, and not in a good way.

'Aren't I just the same?'

My lifelong tendency towards self-centredness had also been fuelled by a hunger for whatever smoothed the way, be it drugs, drink, money, food, safety or shelter. As a homeless man I'd always needed something, and since I was either unable or unwilling to provide it for myself, I had no qualms about taking it from others. There are many different ways that could manifest: stealing from people, lying to them, manipulating them or deceiving them. I'd done it all and had the receipts to prove it.

Although I had repented and committed through action to be a better man than the Gregory who lived in the forest, I was conscious that I kept putting myself first, not only to survive but to flourish in the new life I was building. So how could that be wrong? In cogitating on what the Kiwi had said, it finally dawned on me that being selfish and being self-centred are not the same thing. Not even close.

Because it's almost always used in the pejorative sense, 'selfishness' gets a bad rap in society. (When was the last time you heard someone being commended for being selfish?) I take the opposite view. There's no way I could have become the stable, contented and productive member of society I am today without being selfish. By selfish, I mean understanding what is best for me and prioritising it in the important decisions that guide my life.

I would never have gotten sober or drug free, for instance, had I not acted selfishly. By rejecting invitations to get on the drink or float away on the tip of a needle or the wet end of a joint, I prioritised 'self' over the crabs who wanted to pull me back into the bucket. I wouldn't be where I am professionally had I not selfishly devoted myself to education to the exclusion of just about everything else at the time. Steadfastly refusing to put myself in vulnerable situations in the years since has cemented in me an overriding attitude of selfishness.

It still sounds bad, doesn't it? Well, have a think about what self-*centredness* would have looked like. Giving in to the cravings and blaming some nuns or my parents for it. Finding a stranger to bash in order to provoke my own self-serving pain. Ignoring my family for eternity and resenting them for it. You get the idea.

It was only through attending to myself in a spirit of improvement that I could understand Gregory Peel Smith better and develop him into a person who is loving, mindful, empathetic and caring – the polar opposite of self-centred. Not that being selfish is purely altruistic. In addition to prioritising self-protection, nurturing and self-improvement, selfishness is also about doing what gives me pleasure. Providing help to another human being gives me pleasure. Imparting positive feelings makes me feel contented. Working to help improve the lives of others presses my buttons in a good way. It might not always be obvious to me when I do these things, but they are downright selfish, and that's okay.

It was while I was waking up to this new way of thinking that I discovered I needed to be selfish for two.

For the longest time I was haunted by my past. Running from it was very painful and exhausting, but whenever I stopped running and tried to hide instead, it felt like I only existed in the shadows. The only way I could live in the light was to stop running, turn around and face my problems. When I finally did, barely a day passed when I wasn't confronted with a reason to be anxious.

'What am I afraid of today?'
'What's haunting me today?'

I wasn't really surprised to discover that a great many anxieties emanated from my childhood home: memories of my father belting me, memories of hiding in my room, visions of my sisters screaming or my mother in a blind rage.

Through practising acceptance, forgiveness, mindfulness and being accountable, I gradually came to understand that I didn't create any of that. Since none of it was my fault, there was no need to feel guilty or ashamed. That was a huge relief.

As I worked through each painful past episode, they became less present in my thoughts and less potent in my soul. The traumas faded a little more each year and nowadays they are mostly mere bad memories. During my long resurrection I realised I was transitioning from being a victim to having *been* a victim – an incredibly important metamorphosis. Today as an ageing man I feel liberated from the past, but I still have to take special care of myself, primarily because I know there will always be a part of me that struggles to be contented.

It was during wretched nights beside the fire and hollow days staring into the gullies of Goonengerry that I first became aware of the little boy who lives inside me. He'd poke his head above the parapet now and then, and in my near constant state of inebriation I would shambolically attempt to communicate, only to send him scurrying back into the shadows of my mind. Although he could be elusive and I struggled to connect with him, I knew he was always in there. And I knew he was in pain.

At the end of my great sickness, as light began to spill into my inner world, I started reaching out to him. Sobriety was a big help in clearing the channels of communication, even if I did all the talking. One of the first tangible steps I took to form a bond was to buy my inner child a gift, just to say 'G'day' and acknowledge his existence. I found the perfect present for him one Sunday morning while setting up my market stall at the PCYC, though it's probably more accurate to say the present found me.

A fellow marketeer approached me with a box full of items to sell. Among her knick-knacks was a gold ring in the shape of a teddy bear. I had never seen one before, nor have I since. We haggled for a while before she agreed to let me have it for $21. It might have only cost around the same as a serve of fish and chips, but the ring has become a priceless investment.

The piece of jewellery was diminutive, but I was so thin at the time that it easily slipped onto my left pinkie, where it remains stuck fast today. Later that evening, after the market had ended and I was alone in the sand dunes, I studied it closely and meditated on what it meant. The gold was significant because it represented the value I placed on the relationship with my inner child. The teddy bear shape was a symbol for the sense of love and security I'd never felt as a little boy. That *we'd* never felt.

'I'm giving this to you in recognition of who you are,' I whispered inwardly as dusk folded around my camp. 'I acknowledge your existence: I see you and I know you are worthwhile. I want you to have this ring as a promise that I will be here for you for all our days to come.'

I wasn't expecting a dialogue or a great moment of healing: it was more of a call into the shadows, an outstretched hand to a part of me that will always need one. 'I'm stepping up and I'm willing to develop this relationship with you, but you need to help as well,' I continued. 'I can't do all the work. I can talk to you, but you need to communicate with me as well.'

We left it at that for a while.

It was another few years before I truly got to know him. The breakthrough came in 2005 after I learned about the existence of the Senate's report into the Forgotten Australians. Reading it was a harrowing experience: it validated the abhorrence of my childhood. I was dragged back forty-odd years to when I was a bruised and bleeding victim of domestic violence, an orphan caught in the gears of the Catholic 'care' machine, a brutalised juvenile inmate and an unwanted Ward of the State. I hadn't wept like that since the day in 1965 when my sisters were separated from me at St Patrick's.

Prior to reading that report, any hurt I felt from the past I carried with me as an adult. Opening the pages of the *Forgotten Australians*, however, was akin to stripping my adult self away and finally revealing the boy those things had happened to. I immediately understood that it was *his* hurt causing me residual pain. Although I had always known I was severely damaged, I now knew where that suffering belonged: it belonged with me as a child.

This realisation created a very helpful and clear distinction between my inner child and the adult I had become. It allowed me to look at the damage I had done to myself as an adult in a different way to the damage others had done to me as a child. *I* was responsible for this damage over here, but others were responsible for that damage over there – damage done to the boy.

I could own what I did to myself, accept it and do my best to repair and rebuild. As for the child, I was forced to recognise that there were things I could control and accept and there were things that were beyond my influence. While I couldn't change the fact that other people and other systems had damaged him, I *could* control the way the child understood that.

At the time he was very afraid, timid, subjugated and traumatised to the point of not having a voice. I understood

I had to be the one to hear him and parent him, and I am still doing that today. I have learned that if I don't take care of the child inside me, he can be very mischievous. If I don't give him the attention he needs, he will sabotage me.

In some situations, for example, I will hear words come out of my mouth that haven't been processed by my adult filtering system. They could be in the form of a childish smart-arsed remark or an observation that really shouldn't be made, like when someone trips over or misses a step. Sometimes he'll come out with a silly joke at completely inappropriate times.

> *'How do you catch a rare rabbit?'*
> *'Unique up on it.'*

Sometimes I become aware that there's a nursery rhyme playing in my head. It's the boy inside singing to himself. Although I'm pushing seventy and he's stuck between one and fifteen, we have a lot in common. He also loves animals of any kind, he's mesmerised by people dancing and he's always soothed by the tumbling rain.

In the eighteen years since we first connected it's been important that I regularly spend an appropriate amount of time with that child – *for* that child. Generally speaking,

I'll take time out every few days to just sit with him for a while: maybe we'll have an ice cream, watch a Marvel movie or just have a silly conversation and a few treats.

On those occasions I put the child's needs first. I'm self-ish for him. The adult in me would normally say, 'No, you can't have any more sugar. You can't eat half a tub of ice cream. You can't do this, you can't do that.' But that's not how I want to parent him, for both of our sakes. If I start putting arbitrary limitations on that child, he will rebel. It's far better for me to accept that he needs to be nurtured with a few little treats and some ridiculous moments. We get on much better that way.

I can't speak for the human race, but I suspect many of us are aware of the child within us to some degree, particularly those who have suffered difficulties in their formative years. If my experience is any guide, having a relationship with those lost children is important in developing overall emotional maturity.

The child I'm working with is very damaged, so I need to account for that in our interactions. Just because I have come to terms with most of what's happened to me on an adult level, it doesn't mean the child is always contented. Every now and then he is re-exposed to hurt and I need to address it.

An example of this occurred around 2014–15 when I was interviewing other Forgotten Australians about their experiences for my PhD. The thesis explored the effect that institutional childhood abuse had on care leavers in adult life. Many of those I spoke to shared some utterly heart-breaking stories that affected me deeply – bordering on the vicarious trauma the university had been so concerned about. I was keenly aware, however, that the hurt was being felt by the boy in the back of my mind, not the grown man with the notebook and tape-recorder.

Today he gets upset whenever I see someone in pain. If I read news reports about children being abused, I can feel him squirming: he has empathy with the suffering of others and he wants me to go and save the whole world, which of course I can't do. I have to quietly point out to him that there are things I can control and things I cannot.

On days like that, I have a failsafe tactic to calm him because I know he loves our hens – particularly when they're chicks. If we've had a treat and a chat and he's still not contented, I'll take him down to the back of the yard and spend a bit of time with the ladies as they fuss about and maybe let us take a couple of eggs. That pacifies him. He's always okay after that.

Our relationship has not been a one-way street. Getting to know him has helped me understand what a parent is.

When my daughter, Katie, was born I really had no idea what good parenting involved, other than a recognition that having a father and mother is hugely important. When I first met Catherine thirty-two years later, I suddenly found myself as a role model for her boys, Jackson, who was eleven then, and Charlton, who was eight.

In cautiously stepping into that sacred family space, I resolved selfishly not to put any pressure on myself and only committed to being honest with the boys. I did however look to my inner child for guidance. Whenever issues arose in the home, I would defer to his more sensitive judgement:

'If I were eight or eleven and I had a problem, what would I like to happen?'
'What words would I like to hear from an adult if I was in a difficult situation?'

Getting to know my inner boy led to a significant change in me: I'd identified that I was more than what you just see now. I realised I run far deeper than the academic, the survivor and the lived experience expert. My inner child helped me develop relational wellbeing, not just between the two of us, but between me and every person who is important in my life.

CHAPTER TEN

CONTENTMENT

The multitude of malfunctions that lay at the heart of my tumultuous life had always made romantic relationships difficult for me, if not impossible. The abuse I suffered at the hands of older females in St Patrick's Orphanage scarred me and left me wary of the opposite sex, while drugs, alcohol and poor mental health didn't help me make much sense of intimacy either.

In six decades on the planet, I never once pursued a romance, nor chose to be in a relationship – I just tumbled into them when fate tilted the floor that way. I muddled through without much of a clue about what to do. It's little wonder my marriage to Julie was measured in weeks instead of years or decades, and that my relationship with Katie's mother, Nicola, went up in a bonfire of toxic emotions that scattered us to the four winds.

I had other relationships along the way – some fleeting, others more substantial – but I was never remotely comfortable in them. Only in recent years have I come to understand at least part of the reason why: I had erected an emotional barrier around my heart in an act of self-protection. I was so fearful of being wounded further that getting close to me was pretty much out of the question. The cornerstone of that inner wall was laid on the day Mum delivered us to the orphanage. The logic was, 'If my own mother can hurt me like that, anyone can.'

After largely rebuilding my life, I resolved in 2017 not to bother with relationships ever again. I was happy to focus on being a good man, a hard worker, a good friend and grateful to be alive. After all, I'd worked extremely hard to turn my life into one that was worth living. I had carved out a place in the world, a vocation, a career and a purpose. I had good friends and I'd reconnected with my long-lost sisters and my beautiful daughter. I still had ups and downs, but my baseline was one of deep contentment.

With no partner in my life, I was unsure whether that emotional wall even remained part of my psyche: I had kind of leapt over it already. Although I'd been daunted by the thought of sharing my life story with the world, the publication of my memoir in 2018 was less painful than I expected. The book was well received, and I suddenly found myself in demand for interviews right across the country and internationally. While I was painfully self-conscious about the attention (and still am), I was also blown away by the level of interest it created. I continue to field calls about it today from all around the world.

In 2019 I received a request from closer to home. A lady named Elizabeth Tickle – publisher and editor of *Regional Lifestyle Magazine* – wanted to know if I'd be interested in doing an interview for her publication. She'd seen *Australian Story* and read my memoir, and promised me she'd put an empathetic and talented writer on the case. 'She's on leave at the moment and won't be back for a little while,' Elizabeth added. 'Would it be okay if I have her contact you when she returns?'

'If she's empathetic and talented, then how can I say no?' I consented.

About a week later, I was at home in my solar shack at Lanitza when I received a phone call from one Catherine

Player, top reporter from *Regional Lifestyle Magazine*. After a quick exchange of pleasantries, she said she'd been moved by my book and was eager to find out more about my journey from 'sociopath' to social scientist. By then – years after I struggled to even speak to shopkeepers – I'd grown more comfortable discussing my life. We made an appointment to do an interview over the phone the following Saturday.

When the Friday night rolled around, however, a profusely apologetic Catherine called to ask if it was okay if we postponed the interview. She had just discovered her recording equipment was kaput (this was pre-pandemic and thus pre-Zoom for most of the population). 'I'll get a new recorder and get back to you as soon as possible,' Catherine promised. 'I'm really sorry, I know your time is precious.'

'Yeah, that's alright,' I replied. 'Postponing once is okay, but if you do it again I'll consider you to be unprofessional.'

That remark didn't exactly land with Catherine as I had intended – a garden variety example of me coming across as awkward and unwittingly offensive. To me it was just a statement of fact! I didn't find out until later that Catherine had been completely taken aback. Indeed, she wondered if I was 'an arrogant pig'. When we finally started our interview the following week, I had no idea she slightly hated my guts. Such was the level of her professionalism.

As had become my custom, I had no expectations when I agreed to speak to one of *Regional Lifestyle Magazine*'s top reporters, least of all that I would find the virtual stranger at the other end of the phone to be an excellent, stimulating, intelligent, warm and humorous conversation partner. We'd agreed to do a half-hour interview, but three hours after I answered her call we were still chatting – about some fairly deep and personal subjects, too. I couldn't speak for Catherine, but such a marathon conversation was highly out of character for me. It was certainly the longest I had ever spoken to a complete stranger.

We were only getting started. Our discussion rebooted the following day when Catherine called for a 'supplementary interview', and then again the day after until we ended up calling each other every single day for a month. Although my only experience of Catherine was her voice in my ear, I found myself missing her in between our calls. As soon as we'd hang up, I'd look forward to the next daily dose of D&M.

These weren't interviews, of course; they were the beginnings of something else. At the very least I looked like I'd be welcoming a new friend into my life. Although Catherine and I clearly had a lot in common, we disagreed on plenty, too – and not just about what constitutes professional behaviour.

She was thoughtful and well read, and she was honest and forthright in expressing strong views and opinions. She thought, for example, that I had been fairly harsh towards my mother in *Out of the Forest*, considering the fact Mum had suffered domestic violence right alongside me. It was food for thought, and I continue to reflect on the observation today.

I came to relish the challenge of conversation and respectful disagreement with Catherine. It excited me. While much of my story had been laid bare in a book, Catherine was willing to open the doors of her inner life to me, too. She told me she was separated and raising two young boys in a co-parenting arrangement with their father. Like me, she had grown up in a New South Wales country town west of the Great Dividing Range. She had a background in accounting and education, but her passion – aside from being a dedicated mum – was for the arts. In addition to being a talented writer and painter, Catherine said she was never happier than when onstage singing in bands.

I grew more and more intrigued by this interesting person at the end of the phone, but also a little wary. Was this thing between us becoming something more? After some quiet reflection, I recognised I had indeed lowered my emotional barrier just enough to let Catherine in, but I was worried about something else I'd learned about her – her age. Catherine is twenty-three years my junior: definitely nothing to sneeze at. Still, following a month of intense daily conversation, I thought the respectful thing to do – and an obvious next step in our friendship – was to go and visit her.

Catherine and the boys lived in Orange in Central Western New South Wales, a good ten-hour haul from my joint up at Lanitza. In late 2019, just as the disastrous Black Summer bushfires were beginning to scorch the state, I visited friends on the South Coast of New South Wales and was due to stop and see my Aunty Desley on the Central Coast on my way back home. I figured I could easily swing inland, over the Great Divide and out to Orange on the return trip to finally meet Catherine face-to-face. I hadn't paid much attention to the map: Orange turned out to be a long way off course.

The state was in the grip of drought, and as I drove through the gate of Catherine's property, a great cloud of dust billowed up and swallowed my car. My two little dogs jumped out and ran around in circles, and as I picked them up and walked tentatively towards the house, the door opened and a very beautiful, very young-looking woman stepped out to greet me. When Catherine extended her arms and gave me a gentle hug, I wasn't quite sure how to react. Apparently I was hesitant and awkward (surely not!), but that didn't convey how I felt – I was truly delighted to meet her.

The dogs scurried inside her house and inspected all the rooms before doing some more circle work and finally making themselves at home on the couch. I noticed Catherine's eyes nervously tracking the little critters around her home, but she didn't tell me until days later that she's chronically allergic to dogs.

Somehow Catherine managed not to have a full-blown sneezing fit as we spent the next few hours together. Knowing I'm vegetarian, she made us a goat's cheese and broccoli frittata and we quickly fell into our usual in-depth conversation, devoid of surface banter. Since we'd communicated only via phone up until that point, our burgeoning relationship had nothing to do with looks, sexual attraction or age. From the very beginning it was grounded purely on a human connection and a desire to hear each other's stories.

Since I had a five-hour drive back to the coast and my appointment with Aunty Desley, I finally rounded up the dogs and we said our goodbyes. We shared another hug, a bit more easily for me this time, and as I climbed into my car Catherine handed me a care pack for the road: two boiled eggs, some mung beans and a bread roll. 'There are plenty of service stations on the way,' she said, 'but I don't fancy your chances of finding any vego food in them.'

Meeting in person – in my case with a gorgeous younger woman, and in her case a pretty weathered old bloke – clearly put the 'friendship' on another level. Although we both remained cognisant of the age gap between us, we kept up our daily routine of phone calls and text messages. Communication became so intimate that I felt compelled to ask Catherine, 'Are you flirting with me?'

'NO!' she texted back, followed by silence. I had gotten to know Catherine, however, and I was pretty sure she was flirting, no matter how shocked and offended she tried to come across. Twenty minutes later my phone pinged with an incoming text:

'Okay, in response to your question, the answer is "probably,"' she wrote, *'but I'm not very good at it.'*

She and I both. I guess that's why I'd needed to ask the question in the first place. Now that it was out in the open, our conversations took on a decidedly romantic feel. It was inevitable that we'd be drawn back together.

Two weeks later we hatched a plan to meet up for a weekend in the Blue Mountains – around a two-hour drive for Catherine and an eight-hour trip for me. On the long road south I was slightly dismayed when a negative voice piped up from the past.

'I bet she doesn't even turn up!'
'You're gonna be stuck down there by yourself, embarrassed.'
'Maybe I should turn around now.'

Had I met Catherine a few years earlier, those internal party poopers might well have won the day, but I had come too far to be so easily derailed by self-doubt. I did a quick scan of the emotional terrain in search of signs of resistance – any indication that I was going down the wrong path. Aside from the nagging concern about my age, I felt nothing but a warm wind in my hair urging me to keep going.

I'd taken on the task of booking an Airbnb in the beautiful mountain township of Blackheath. Half an hour after I arrived, on Valentine's Day, 2020, Catherine pulled into the driveway and literally ran from her car. This hug was different – electrically charged – and it was followed by a kiss. This was a huge moment for us – a huge moment for *me*! My emotional wall had turned to dust and for the first time in my life, at the tender age of sixty-four, I chose to be in a relationship.

The weekend was a time of deep and complete connection. I have always struggled with love, what it is, what it's meant to feel like and definitely how to describe it. I am learning that a part of love is wanting to be in someone's life forever. To feel the pain they experience. To see them when they are not looking, and observe how beautiful they are in each moment – inside and out. To want to be a part of their new stories, and to create memories together to be reviewed later with a laugh and a smile, and maybe even a tear.

Our first weekend together was all about the laughs. The Airbnb I'd chosen was slightly odd but lovely – provided you didn't mind hanging out with a bunch of dead cats. When we first walked in we were both freaked out to find four taxidermied felines on display, just standing there and staring weirdly into space. It wasn't until later that Catherine revealed, jokingly, that her first thought was, 'Holy shit! Is this guy going to kill me? Is this how it ends?'

Not a chance, and since they were all frozen in time, the pet cemetery didn't pose an allergy issue to her either. To top off the strangeness, the owner had left strict instructions: 'Please don't pat the cats!'

As if anyone in their right mind would.

Catherine duly named the place 'the Kooky Cat' and when we closed the door to the rental on a sunny Sunday afternoon, we did a slow dance in the courtyard and committed to spending the rest of our lives together. When we hugged one last time, Catherine whispered in my ear, 'I don't think I can let you go.' I knew exactly how she felt.

On the drive home, I knew I had just stepped through a major door in my life. It was at once exciting, terrifying and daunting. For all the emotional safety, friendship, shared humour, attraction and mutual trust we'd built up, the fact remained that I was sixty-four and Catherine was forty. She was also raising two boys on her own. As I motored back up the Pacific Highway, the ol' voice started up again:

> 'What happens if I run out of energy?'
> 'What if I get to seventy-five and keel over?'
> 'Will the boys accept the relationship?'
> 'Will they resent me?'

All I could do was remain in the very centre of the three-day week and be honest, decent and mindful. Although we had some concerns about our age difference, Catherine was a calm voice of reason. 'We can only take each step together as it comes,' she counselled me. 'I know my boys, and I know they will accept you.'

*

Ever since I bought land at Lanitza and erected my little tin castle, I have tried to have flowers in bloom there all year round. I leave buckets of water about the place, too, because I get a kick out of watching birds dunking themselves and playing in them. I take time to commune with the little tortoises that live in my dam, the reptiles and marsupials that roam the grounds, and my darling chooks, who are safe and sound inside their own wire citadel.

As much as I love the animals, though, I'm a complete sucker for flowers. I plant daisies, pansies, agapanthus, gladiolas and whatever else I can get to grow in the warm oceanic climate. They're beautiful and their colours turn me on in the most pleasant way. The flowers aren't only for me, though: I love what they provide for other creatures, too – food, shelter and nectar in ancient symbiosis.

Over the years I've tried to add even more to the rambling gardens around my shed. Specifically, I have a thing for tulips, jonquils and daffodils, but my repeated attempts to grow them have wilted and died under the full glare of the subtropical sun.

I had long split my time between the shack at Lanitza and my little rented unit in Coffs Harbour, but when COVID-19 arrived – just as Catherine and I departed the Kooky Cat – I was very fortunate that the virus changed the way we work in society. Almost overnight, lecture theatres were emptied and university campuses were shuttered. Thankfully technology allowed us to teach online, which meant I could work from anywhere with an internet connection. In March 2020 I took a deep breath, loaded up the car and relocated 750 km away to Orange to live with Catherine and the boys.

A lot has happened in the three years since, but I quickly found, to my persistent delight, that Orange has the perfect climate for growing tulips, jonquils and daffodils. Although I took it as a sign, the path forward wasn't exactly scattered with petals.

Stepping into an established family is terrifying, especially when you haven't had good role models in your life. It's even freakier when your only sense of family ended at age ten and you'd worked hard to accept you'd probably never, ever be in a family again. Until I fell in love with Catherine, such an outlandish idea had never even crossed my mind.

Not only had I entered an intimate domestic relationship with Catherine – in her house – I was suddenly a presence in the lives of Jack and Charlton: energetic and fast-developing lads who have a close relationship with their dad. To say it was an intensely difficult adjustment is an understatement – it was like learning to walk and breathe on an alien planet.

Two weeks after landing on it, I was back at Lanitza. I needed to get away to decompress and think things through. It was the selfish thing to do.

'How do I approach this?'
'Am I really going to be able to be in this family? It's a huge responsibility – the biggest thing there is.'
'What would be the best thing for everyone?'

With no functioning understanding of family life, I could only fall back on what I had learned about life since leaving the forest. The first order of business remained the same as when I walked away from the park bench: do no harm. Primarily, that meant doing no harm to the boys' sense of safety and normality. I didn't try to push myself on them or feign that I was something I am not, least of all their father.

Step two was to take it slowly and practise. In the early days, I needed to get away quite often. I'd travel the well-worn road back to Lanitza every second weekend to spend time watching the birds and assess how I was managing with family life and the huge responsibility that goes with it. With each trip away I developed more acceptance and confidence. I'd recommit to working at our new arrangement, just as Catherine did, in the belief that we'd eventually work through the teething problems. To her enduring credit, Catherine was very patient with me.

As is often the way with me, overcoming the worries was aided by the wisdom I found in clichés. The first: 'Feelings aren't always facts.'

Even though I 'felt' uncomfortable trying to fit into the family, the 'fact' was I could walk away at any time, should I wish to. So what was I going to invest in? Feelings or facts? I chose the feelings: to confront my discomfort and work through it because I could see the long-term reward: spending the rest of my life with Catherine. My love for her – another 'feeling' – was already well established so I had a solid foundation to build on.

The other cliché I took comfort in was an age-old line I'd heard muttered in soup kitchens many times over the years: 'This, too, shall pass.'

Whenever I felt overwhelmed, lost or unsure of my place in the family or the world, I reminded myself that what-ever problem I faced was only temporary. Hell, just to get to where I was, I had already overcome alcoholism, addic-tion, poverty, homelessness, mental illness, unemployment, disease, trauma and self-loathing. As long as I strived to be the best person I could, and if I didn't place any expectations on myself or others, the canoe would carry me forward.

In those early days I reflected a lot on the makeshift diagram I'd drawn in the forest. In becoming a newly minted and highly underqualified 'family man', I occasionally spiked through the outer lines, but over a period of two years – having brought all of my post-epiphany learnings to bear – I found myself more often than not within the comfortable zone of contentment. When I reflect on that period now, I have few regrets and mostly lovely memories.

When I first arrived in Orange, Jack and Charlton wanted to go for lots of walks in the local conifer forest. When I think back on those hikes I remember massive red mushrooms with white spots, helping the boys pick out the different birdsongs, breathing the cool pine air and feeling relaxed and grounded in the company of my loving partner.

From then on, whenever we'd set off on adventures, I'd remind the boys – as much as I'd remind myself – that we were going to have memories of the day. 'Let's make them good ones!' I'd jolly them. 'That way when we look back in years to come, we'll have good things to talk about.' I had no fond memories from my childhood and I was damned if I was going to miss out a second time around.

Family life began to fill me up in other ways, too. In some respects Catherine is very traditional. She likes us all to be around the dining table at mealtimes. That's something else I never experienced as a boy, and I absolutely love it. Straight away I could see it was sacred family time: time for news, time for the day's achievements and special moments to be discussed.

I've been delighted to learn how family life can shape a person's habits and character, too. Now, as the boys are getting older, their lifestyles are changing a little bit. If Charlton has an early dinner, the first thing he does is set himself a place at the table. Same with Jack, and they'll always sit at the table for their breakfast. It is the nerve centre of household communications, and I can see they love being plugged into it. So do I.

Jack's closing in on his senior high school years and is fairly busy with study, a job, football and friends. Charlton's not far off a more independent phase too, but his smiling face is still pretty visible around the house and he's my number-one go-to and helper with the chooks. Often when he comes home from school he'll join me down at the coop and help me potter around with the ladies, spread a bit of mulch and hay around and sometimes he'll make an interesting discovery. Recently he noticed one of the chooks had laid an egg without a shell. He shot me a conspiratorial look. 'That's the topic for dinner tonight,' he said.

Yep, there's always something to discuss around that big wooden table and lately we've been setting a place for one more.

William Peel Player-Smith – otherwise known as William the Thirsty – was born at 3.25 pm on 4 August 2022.

Becoming a father again has opened a stunning new chapter in my life. It has provided me with fresh perspectives, a greater understanding of the human condition and the opportunity to learn more about love, sharing, destiny and contentment.

In a way, welcoming William at Orange Base Hospital also took me back in time, to 1986 when Katie was born. I will always mourn the lost time with her as I teetered on the brink of self-destruction. Today I am a different man, but it isn't lost on me that William's arrival also has a time component that relates to me. I've had to confront the existential question, 'How long will I live to be his father?'

I don't know, of course, and I can only do my very best to extend my time through clean living, a good diet, exercise and having a healthy and active mind. I know what having an elderly father will ultimately mean to William and that will be up to him to negotiate, but I don't plan on going anywhere soon and I know he will never be alone. His mother, brothers and sister adore him, and he's cherished by a large circle of aunts, uncles, cousins and a doting grandma in Catherine's mum.

Adding William to the household has required some adjustments to the way we do things. Aside from the huge footprint that tiny people make with their pram, playpen, cot, bottles, bunny rugs, car seat, change table, nappies and toys, William has caused me to adjust my outlook as a role model. As soon as he was born, I wanted Charlton and Jack to feel secure and assured them that I saw no difference between them and their baby brother. I promised I would never discriminate or ask them to do anything I wouldn't ask William to do, too.

While the concept of love is something I struggled to comprehend for more than fifty years, I never expected I would do a three-year crash course on the subject late in life. I have come to understand that, above all, love is unconditional in the family. I believe that under the auspices of love, all conversations can be had. Under the auspices of love, better understandings can evolve.

Love comes down to the little things as well as the big stuff. Love means truly sharing the relationship. It's about allowing your partner the time and space to do what they need to do, whether it involves you or not. Love is about sharing workloads and chores. It's stepping up, taking responsibility and mopping the floor at 10 o'clock at night even though you don't want to. It's about doing the things you don't want to see your partner do. I chop the wood and make sure there's enough kindling to make the fire easy to start. Love goes around and it comes around. Catherine has introduced me to a better wardrobe, not for her but for me, and I know if she is baking me scones, she's doing it because she loves me too.

Love is planning for the future. One of our objectives is to leave a good legacy for the three boys, and we work towards fulfilling that goal every day. In my case I have to do it twice as fast as most, because I'm twice as old. But, as ever, the journey is the reward. Since I still work mostly from home, I am as hands-on with William as any stay-at-home parent. I've been right by his side as he's slowly morphed from a slightly premature newborn into a happy, giggling baby. It's a privilege to be on the journey with him.

I love holding him, feeding him, listening to him and watching him sleep. I know we're going to make memories together and I'm determined that they will be good ones, because one day he'll lean on them a lot. Lately, however, we've discovered a mutual love of cartoons, even though we come at it from uncommon angles. I like the goofy characters and silly plotlines, while William seems more enamoured of the bright colours, moving pictures and the playful music. His mouth hangs agape as his big eyes absorb it all. It doesn't matter that we take different things from the experience, what counts is that we're at one in the moment together: William, me, and the little boy inside.

POSTSCRIPT

'So are you happy?'

I've had to get used to fielding a lot more questions in recent years – not just in detox and rehab centres but from students, colleagues, governments, medical and social support agencies and members of the public. It's almost as if society has gone overboard to compensate for ignoring me during my homeless years.

For a while, the most persistent questions related to my life as a hermit.

'Did you make a hut or something?' (No.)

'Were you lonely?' (Only sometimes.)

'Do you miss it?' (Very, very rarely.)

'What does bat taste like?' (It tastes like bat, but better with a few spices.)

Although I still find the attention hard to handle, I'm happy to answer people's questions; after all, I did invite intrigue by writing a book about it. One query that comes up a lot is whether I kept any souvenirs from the rainforest. If, by that, people mean a pebble from the creek, a rock from my campfire, a walking stick from a gum tree or some other terrestrial totem, the answer is no. Aside from ten years' worth of strange, sad, powerful, beguiling and fantastical memories, I left the forest with nothing but the tattered clothes I was wearing, a didgeridoo and my small canvas dilly bag.

The dilly bag was extremely important to me. It hung off my shoulder wherever I went and it contained what I thought were the essentials for life: tobacco, any drugs I happened to have, a pocketknife, a hash pipe, cigarette papers, a candle, matches, a safety pin, a pencil and a small sack of marbles. The safety pin was a hangover from my heroin days. Part of my addiction was for the feeling of a needle slipping under the skin. For years afterwards when the long, cold fingers of craving clawed at me, I'd get the safety pin out and draw blood on my forearms to placate the old addict within. Nowadays it's just a handy fastener.

As for the marbles, I picked them up at a community market stall in Mullumbimby in the mid-nineties just so

I could say that, no matter what happened, at least I still had my marbles. Boom-boom! It was half true because there were times I thought I might be going mad up there on the mountaintop in Goonengerry.

I still have the dilly bag today, and it still goes everywhere with me. However, only the safety pin, pencil, pocketknife and the marbles remain from my old life. Although it hasn't happened for a while, I have experienced episodes of latent dissociation in my later life and had to reach for the marbles to centre myself again.

All of the other crap I didn't need, so I replaced it with items that have helped me recover from shame and stigma and remind me what direction I'm heading in. Symbolism is very important to me so, along with a beautiful bird's feather I found in the sand dunes during my early days studying at TAFE, I've added:

A tape measure (to ensure I measure up as a man).
A small spirit level (to remind me of the value of honesty).
A Leatherman multi-tool (just because it's a useful bit of gear).
A cigarette lighter (after years surviving beside a fire, it is hugely important to me).

A torch (to find my way in the dark).

A small wooden spoon (I half-jokingly tell people it signifies my tendency to be a stirrer, but the truth is that I bought it for the child within. No matter where I go, I can pick up a little tub of ice cream, bust out the spoon and take time out to share a treat).

In short, the dilly bag is full of reminders that finding contentment takes thought, mindfulness, planning, self-reflection, patience and vigilance.

Following my TEDx Talk in 2021 – which crammed my life's journey into a twenty-minute speech – I found myself bombarded with questions that weren't so much about living in a rainforest as they were about me.

'What is your greatest regret?' came up a lot.

I can honestly say I don't have any: not a single one. Not anymore. Before I began the journey of healing I had so many regrets I could hardly shoulder them. Where my regret involved other people, I have sought them out and apologised and, if necessary, made reparations. I'm pretty confident I have now reached a point where I've run out of people and run out of regrets.

'What is your proudest achievement?' is another crowd favourite.

There have been a lot of big moments. Walking away from the park bench was a huge one – maybe the biggest. Gaining entry into university is way up there, too, as is getting first-class Honours, winning a scholarship and attaining a PhD. Gaining friends and making a life with Catherine and the boys has also been enormous. While those things allowed me to feel a certain amount of satisfaction, the achievement I'm most proud of is simply living a stable, contented life for the past twenty-odd years. It has definitely been the most rewarding, too.

When I first left the backpack full of booze and drugs behind, I had no idea where life would lead me – only that it had to be better than the way I was living. Never did I think I would one day be an author. Although, during my early days living in the forest, before I broke through rock bottom and landed in hell, I had a cool idea for a book. It came to me after I caught a glimpse of my reflection in the creek near my campsite. Although looking at myself was something I had avoided my entire life, on this day it didn't sting so much and the sight of my face peering back at me got me thinking. As I sat beside the fire later that evening, I imagined a beautiful leather-bound cover embossed with the title 'Self Help: Everything You Need to Know is Inside'. Instead of pages with words, however, it would simply open to a mirror.

I think the book you're holding now might be the closest I get to seeing that idea come to fruition. I encourage you to look in the mirror, too, and have a good look around deep within. There's contentment in there, I promise you. You just have to go in and find it.

Dr Gregory P. Smith
April 2023

ACKNOWLEDGEMENTS

To my treasured family. A huge thank you to Catherine, who encouraged me, fussed over me and supported me through many late nights as this book slowly took shape. A big shout out, too, to the fine young men of the household, Jackson and Charlton, who stoically took on extra kitchen duties to free up time for me to think and write. It meant a lot to me, fellas. Finally a special nod to the little man, William, just because he's gorgeous.

And to Craig Henderson, my very good friend and co-writer, who has been magnificent in helping to structure the content and turn my words into beautiful prose. I thank him.

RESOURCES

If you're in need of some help or if you find yourself troubled by the contents of this book, please reach out and talk to someone.

Lifeline
Crisis support and suicide prevention services
lifeline.org.au
13 11 14

Beyond Blue
Mental health support services for anxiety, depression and suicide
beyondblue.org.au
1300 224 636

1800RESPECT
Confidential information, counselling and support for domestic, family and sexual violence
1800respect.org.au
1800 737 732

Relationships Australia
Relationship support services for individuals, families and communities
relationships.org.au
1300 364 277

MensLine
Relationship advice and mental health support for men
mensline.org.au
1300 78 99 78

National Alcohol and Other Drug Hotline
Free, confidential, 24/7 support for those struggling with addiction or worried about their drug or alcohol use
counsellingonline.org.au
1800 250 015

Suicide Call Back Service
A free nationwide service providing 24/7 phone and online counselling to people affected by suicide
suicidecallbackservice.org.au
1300 659 467

Read on for an extract of *Out of the Forest*

BUSH SPORTS

I was in control in the forest. It was my space, nobody knew it like I did and nobody could ever kick me out. Even if they'd wanted to, they would have to find me first. Plenty of people knew I was living somewhere in the Goonengerry mountains, but no one had any idea exactly where. I know this because they used to come looking for me. I'd always hear them – or smell them – long before they stumbled anywhere near my camp.

Very early on I'd worked out that the key to staying hidden in the bush came down to how well I could control my fire. Smoke was the anathema of secrecy so selecting the right wood to burn at the right time of day was crucial. Dead, hard, very dry wood was the best – essentially a smokeless fuel. Although it burned OK, wet or greenish wood sent up cumulus puffs of white smoke. You might as well drop a pin marker on Google Maps.

On misty or rainy days I could get away with burning a bit of greener fuel because the smoke would melt into the rainforest's natural fog. Keeping a fire going in the rain wasn't that hard, just a matter of leaning a big log over the top of it and stoking the flames underneath. The only other time I'd risk a smoky fire was after dark when it didn't matter. It had the added benefit of keeping the swarming mosquitoes at bay. Besides, I figured anyone who was in the forest at night was there for nefarious purposes and the last thing they wanted was to run into me.

In the event that someone did happen upon my camp, I had a series of secret escape trails. I was at peace with the idea of having to walk away. I was prepared in my mind to just pick up my dillybag and go. That was real freedom, I thought. I called it my Moscow Strategy, in honour of the slash and burn tactic used against Napoleon's army in the defence of Moscow. Until such time I was free to stay and set fire to as much wood as I pleased.

Smoke – but not the campfire variety – was often the first sign that people were looking for me, or at least roaming close. Eau de ciggie carries a long way in the bush and my half-man, half-marsupial nose would twitch at the first distinctive hint of Winfield or Benson & Hedges, even before I heard any voices or blundering footfalls on the forest floor.

I strongly suspect these intrepid explorers were fringe dwellers. They'd have seen me walking along Mill Road towards the main trail; or they'd have eyeballed me in Mullumbimby or Byron Bay, or seen me trudging along on the outskirts of town. It wouldn't have been too hard to make the association. Nine times out of ten it would be a couple of young guys who'd chance their hands and attempt to find the Bearded Bunyip.

I didn't mind at all. In fact, I quite enjoyed it because it gave me something to do. I liked to play games with them, only they didn't realise they were playing. There were a lot of trails in the forest. Some were wide and some narrower, other tracks were barely perceptible and some – the ones that I made – well, you couldn't see them at all. The trick to covering your tracks, I had worked out, was to never walk in a straight line. If I wanted to make a pathway from the creek to my camp, for example, I would never just plough straight into the bush at a right angle to the creek. Such a clumsy approach would be obvious and visible straight away.

Instead, I'd make an oblique path at a thirty-degree angle to the creek. But after five metres or so I'd stop and head back in the opposite direction, still at a thirty-degree angle of progress, for another five metres. Then back and forth and so on until I ended up with a zigzagging track that was completely invisible from the creek. You could be standing right in front of it and never see it. Or I could be hiding in there watching you and you'd never know it.

I could arrange the forest like a human chess board, and my favourite game was designed to mess with the heads of the little pawns who'd come in search of the king. Not unlike the rest of the country, it was a sport played mainly on weekends.

Though I generally never knew what day it was at any given time, I could pick out Saturdays and Sundays or holidays because that's when more people tended to come into the forest. For the most part the mountaintop was tranquil, but on weekends, depending on the time of year, it could get a bit louder. Chainsaws, motorbikes, 4WDs, voices. All the noises that rubbed me up the wrong way.

I'd prepare for their arrival by making big, obvious trails designed to send them away from the vicinity of my camp. On the opposite bank of the creek I'd stomp out obvious tracks that led uphill and deeper into the forest. Once I'd gone, say, twenty metres, I'd stop dead and carefully walk back out. The result was a phantom trail that plunged meaningfully into the heart of the forest and then abruptly stopped dead for no apparent reason.

Whenever people walked down the creek towards my territory, I'd have already put my fire out as a precaution. I'd have heard them coming a mile off – or smelled their ciggies. They'd usually look around a bit, marvel at the view from the top of the waterfall and inevitably spot one of my bogus tracks on the northern side of the creek. I'd sit in a hidey-hole on my side and watch them disappear into the bush. After a while I'd see them stop, bewildered that the trail just ended. Sometimes they'd look straight up at the rainforest canopy. I don't know if they were expecting to see a spaceship or a drop bear but I found it tremendously amusing.

Sometimes, if I was feeling particularly fiendish, I'd whip up a set of baby tracks for the weekend warriors to puzzle over. These were easy to construct and they really screwed with people's minds. I'd make a fist and gently press it into the sand of the creek bank, leaving what looked like the curl of a human foot, only tiny. Using a finger I'd smudge little toe prints near the top and, with alternate hands,

I'd make a trail of little footprints along the length of the creek. Voila! Human baby tracks in the middle of nowhere! Freaky stuff.

It's not surprising, then, that I became the subject of wild rumours and local legend. Not that everyone was fearful of me. One day, after about four or five years, I found a note under a stone near the entrance of the main trail. It was written in pen on a single sheet of lined paper torn from a spiral notebook, and it was addressed to me:

To the Man in the Forest,
I have some accommodation on my property.
You'd be welcome to stay in it for free if you'd like.
It's the first gate on the left as you go down the road.
Please consider it and let me know if you'd be interested.

It gave directions and the address of the property on Mill Road. I knew exactly which one it was. The owner was a guy they called The Professor. He was a university lecturer, but he also had greenhouses in which he grew plants: palms, flowers and all manner of amazing flora.

He lived on a breathtakingly beautiful piece of land – a couple of hundred north-facing acres draped across the eastern side of the mountain. Unbeknown to The Professor, I went on a clandestine property inspection one day while he was at work. In one field, away from the main homestead, I found a roomy caravan with a large glass annexe built on the front of it. I assumed this was what he had in mind for me, and I have to admit it was pretty tempting. I visualised myself sitting in the sun with a joint, gazing all the way out over Brunswick Heads and Byron Bay. You could even see the lighthouse. Quite a domain.

The note had said to consider the offer, so I did. I thought about it for a good six months before I finally decided I'd pass. In the end I realised I didn't want to be obligated to anyone for anything ever, and it was just as well. About a year down the track I learned the reason The Professor had wanted me on his property. A myth had grown about a creepy man who lived in the forest and The Professor had figured if I was living on his land no one would go near it. Apparently he'd been losing plants and other property to thieves and he thought I might make a good guard dog. Thanks, but no thanks.

Perhaps this added to my mystique. The more they couldn't find me, the more people wanted to know who I was. This put me at an advantage, and I was quite happy to feed my own mythology. As with Byron Bay, whenever I went into Mullumbimby I'd usually walk there during the night and already be in town when people started moving about in the morning.

While it gave my reputation an edge, this nocturnal navigation also sharpened my sense of touch beyond anything I thought possible. The tactile sense was the only one I could confirm and trust implicitly in the dark. After a while I found that I could walk through the forest at night with my eyes closed without breaking a spider web – just by feeling my way. I could sense the nanosecond a web brushed against my face and I'd stop, adjust course and keep moving. Whenever people asked me how I was feeling I'd reply, 'With my hands.'

In all those years I never ran into another person in the forest at night. Probably a good thing; I might have scared them to death.

Yet the irony of people being afraid of me was almost comical: after all, I was frightened of them. If an amateur weekend search party *had* managed to find me up there, and maybe turned the tables and watched me through the bushes, perhaps their fears would have been replaced by pity. I was totally alone and my day-to-day life was pathetic. If I wasn't drinking green poison out of a garbage bin for breakfast or eating fistfuls of dope, I was scrounging up firewood and ferns to sleep on, or scraping together meagre rations to eat with my filthy fingers. I'd sit for hours and stare into the canyon while I contemplated the tattered story of my life. The drunker and higher I got, the more I gibbered and mumbled to myself. Not so scary after all, just sad.

In the beginning I occupied myself by setting tasks to pass the time, even if they seemed impossible. For a long time my only tool in the forest was my pocket knife. It had a lovely stainless-steel blade, maybe seven or eight centimetres long, which folded out of the handle. I discovered I could move a two-tonne fallen tree using that knife. I just had to think like an Egyptian.

I read somewhere that the ancient Egyptians had built the pyramids using pretty simple rules of physics and engineering. I didn't have any giant stone edifices to move but there was a massive log near Rome that I'd started to obsess over. It was at the bottom of a long, steep section of the main trail and I became fixated on getting it to the top, simply so I could roll it all the way back down again. The problem was that it was huge – about three metres long and as high as my waist.

Slowly, my inner-Ramses came to the fore. I used the knife to sharpen some smaller branches in order to jam them in under the fallen tree. Using these as levers, I was able to shift one end of the log a little, then wedge in a rock to hold it in place while I went and moved the other end with another stick. Up the hill it went – wedge by wedge, inch by inch. Three days later I stood triumphant at the summit with one foot on the fallen tree like a wrestler standing over a hapless foe. With a thrust of my boot I sent it thudding down the hill, kicking up leaves and clumps of dirt from the trail before it careened off into the bush with a satisfying crunch.

With no TV or even a radio, little projects like this occupied my head and distracted me from my myriad problems. After a few years I guessed it would be worthwhile trying to keep track of time. Rather than buy a watch I looked around the forest. I soon found what I was looking for: a very straight stick of uniform width around fifty centimetres long. I sharpened one end and shoved it into the dirt at one side of my campsite, supporting it with rocks at the base so it wouldn't budge a millimetre.

Although it started as an attempt to make a sun dial, the stick took off on other journeys in my mind. I would watch it every day, and before long was marking the ground around it with little sticks and rocks of different shape and colour. I had rocks to chart the sunset and sunrise, others to mark the zenith of the sun on particular days. Other rocks and sticks related to the moon cycle. I started to plot the solstices and the equinoxes, the changing of the seasons, and I'd mark them out with little stones, too. It ended up being more of a universe dial than a sun dial.

I left that stick in the ground for years. It gave me something to think about, and I didn't have to put a lot of energy into it. All I had to do was stare at it, which became a ritual. But I also became fascinated with the piece of wood itself. If you leave a stick in the ground and watch it for long enough, you'll see it as a tiny pin upon which the entire planet spins.

I played other games, too, with my candles. I constructed little moulds in the dirt and attempted to make different shapes – little animals and the like – by dripping wax into them. Sometimes I'd spend hours simply picking up dirt and separating out the silica. After a few hours I'd end up with just a handful of the sparkling mineral, like Blackbeard of the bush with his treasure. And I would explore. I roamed all over the forest and I knew all of its secrets and riddles.

There was one place, however, that was strictly off limits. Although I often toyed with the idea, I never climbed right down to the bottom of the waterfall into the valley below. I was extremely wary of the cliff top, particularly given how wobbly I'd get on dope and my creek juice. Sometimes I'd clamber down a little way to see how far I could comfortably go, but mostly I treated the cliff with respect. I didn't realise it until later but this showed me that I didn't really want to die.

I also had the fire for entertainment. A good campfire beats a flat-screen TV hands down – even watching

Inspector Gadget on Tryptanol and cones. After a while the fire became more to me than just a bush television and means of cooking and keeping warm – it ended up at the centre of my spirituality. The most incredible things started to happen around my campfire. Amazing conferences and gatherings that would eventually save my life.

Discover a
new favourite

Visit **penguin.com.au/readmore**